# 49 Ways to Make a Living in Sweden

Bob Martin

ISBN-13: 978-1530549177
ISBN-10: 1530549175

# DEDICATION

This book is dedicated to my kids.  Chris, Jean, Aaron, Jared and Nicole. You guys make life worth living.

# Contents

# FOREWORD

Welcome to my newest book, 49 Ways to Make a Living in Sweden. This is actually, more or less, the second major edition of this book. Previously, though, the book was entitled "49 Ways to Make a Living in The Philippines". I am an American who lives in the Philippines and that first edition of this work was focused on other expats who live in the Philippines, how they could make money. So many readers of the book told me that I really should change the title of the book, because the vast majority of the ideas I presented could be used anywhere in the world. This was even said to me by several book reviewers as well.

So, in this new edition, I decided to take that advice. In addition to refocusing on a worldwide audience, I have also updated the ideas that I present, as well as edited some. A few of the ideas that I presented in the first edition were indeed very focused on those expats in the Philippines, so since I was reaching for a larger audience this time around, I decided to eliminate those few ideas that were indeed focused so narrowly.

So, let's look at my ideas. Actually, these are more than mere ideas, because the vast majority of the things that we will discuss are things that I truly have done over my years of being self-employed.

One additional note. The title of this book is **49 Ways to Make a Living in Sweden**. Well, we need to set the ground rules for what exactly a "job" is. For the purposes of this book, let's agree that a "job" is being employed by another person or company. If you are self-employed you are building a business, something of value, not simply punching a time clock. So, I do not consider being self-employed the same as working a job.

# INTRODUCTION

Hi, my name is Bob Martin. I am an American, and I have been self-employed since May 1991. Not every person who is self-employed is truly an entrepreneur, but that is what I am. I suppose I am an entrepreneur to the extreme. Some people have told me that I am a "serial entrepreneur".

My entrepreneurial spirit came alive at an early age, I suppose when I was only 9 or 10 years old. I don't remember for sure, but that is as close as I can get to it. Throughout my life I have been starting new businesses almost as a hobby. At a young age, I had grass cutting businesses, painting businesses, really a business for almost anything you could imagine.

When I was about 30 years old I inherited a substantial amount of money. Like so many who come into money, though, I was wasteful. I used the money in stupid ways, and didn't save it or invest it wisely like I should have. There was a time when I thought that the money I had would last me a lifetime.

I was wrong, though.

I started a few businesses with that money, but I did not apply myself, I was wasteful and inattentive to my businesses, because I thought that my money pit was endless.

Some of those businesses experienced a fair amount of success, but as I continued to pay less attention than I should have, those businesses that started out as a success withered on the vine for the most part.

I had moved from the USA to the Philippines, where life is much cheaper, so I thought that I was set.

To make a long story short, after only 2 years in the Philippines, I was nearly out of money. In my wildest dreams, I didn't expect to be in that position! Well, as you can guess, it was time to do something. Basically, my wife and I came to the conclusion that we either had to learn how to make money here in the Philippines, one of us had to go back to the States to earn money, or we had to pack up the whole family and go back to the States.

There was one thing that I knew for certain. I didn't want to go back to the States. I loved living in the Philippines. I also didn't want Feyma, my wife, to go back and earn money, leaving me and the kids here. We had to stay together as a family. That meant that we had to learn a way to make money while living here. What we were doing was not working.

Our conclusion was that we had to do two things, actually. First, we had to look for ways to increase our income. Secondly, and just as importantly, we had to get our budget under control. Feyma came to me one day and told me:

> *Honey, remember, in the States, you used to do well selling on eBay. Why don't you give it a try from here in the Philippines?*

Well, the thought had actually not occurred to me. When I thought about it, my initial reaction was to dismiss it. Selling online to US customers from the Philippines simply was not feasible! How could I ship goods halfway around the world? Feyma encouraged me, though, and quickly I decided to give it a try. In only a few weeks' time, it became obvious that I could indeed sell on eBay, and do quite well at it! I'll tell you more about that venture later in this book.

Not only did I sell on eBay, I found other ways to make money online! It got to the point where I realized that the way for me to earn a living while living in the Philippines was to not focus on the local market, but rather to market my business toward people outside the Philippines!

Soon, I had built up a number of different websites where I was earning money – good money. I actually got to the point where I was earning more money living here in the Philippines than I ever earned when I lived in the USA. Since that time, I have continued to make changes in my business to fit the changing times. I have closed down some businesses, and I have started a whole lot of new businesses too. One thing, though, I would have to say that every business I have done has enjoyed some success. I don't know of a single business that I've started where I didn't make at least some money. You can do it too.

When I tell people about this, one reaction that is quite common is that people will say that starting a business is expensive, and they don't have enough money to start a business. It is important to keep in mind, though... I am mostly talking about online businesses. If you are talking of starting up a "brick and mortar" business (a business that is a physical entity – a store that you can drive to and walk into) yes, it is expensive. But putting up a business on the web is cheap!

How much do you need to start up a business on the Internet? Well, you need a little money up front, but not too much. I will say that if you spend maybe $200 or so, you can get yourself set up and ready to do business online.

This will be used to buy Domain names, set up hosting online, maybe buy some software needed to get everything going, etc. After you spend that amount (maybe more, but probably not), you can start opening up businesses. That's right, that amount will set you up to where you can open multiple businesses. Maybe you will need to spend a little extra for extra businesses, but very little. Frankly, I have never spent more than $100 to start any online businesses. And, from that $100 investment, I have a number of businesses that have earned me in the area of a half-million dollars each. You can do it too! Just look at the following examples of 49 different business ideas that you can do from the Philippines, where I live, or from anywhere in the world, that will earn you an income (perhaps more than you are earning now!). As a bonus, after going over each of these 49 business ideas, I will have an Appendix section that will go over how I did it. What businesses I did, how they worked out for me and where they stand now.

# SECTION 1 - THE BIGGIES

The best ways if you want to make big money.

# 1 - SELLING ON EBAY

Don't laugh it off, eBay is not just a place to play around, and indeed, you can make real money selling on eBay. eBay is, in my opinion, the most perfect marketplace in the world. One of the things that makes it so good is that it is worldwide! You can make serious money on eBay. I know you can, because I have done it on more than one occasion in my life. When I first got into eBay from here in the Philippines, I was hoping that I could maybe make $1,000 or so per month in profits, and when added to other income that I was making, it should set me up into a nice position. In truth, I was able to refine my eBay selling system to the point where I made many times that amount. I had months where I made up to $30,000 in a single month by simply selling on eBay. And, my least successful months in those days were around $15,000 per month. So, this was not just playing around, this was a serious business!

The key to doing this kind of volume on eBay is that you have to run many auctions simultaneously. It is also important that you find items that you can sell over and over again. In other words, you don't want to have a different item time after time. You want to find items that you can sell identical items over and over again. Why? It's simple, it is a lot less work! Once you set up an item on auction one time, you can set it up to simply re-list itself if (when) it sells. So, the instant that the item sells, an identical item is re-listed. This is the key to making big money on eBay. If you are selling unique items, you have to go in and manually set up a new auction for each individual item you want to sell. You won't have time to do this if you are doing a big volume in sales!

I said that you need to run many auctions at a single time. How many? When I was at my peak on eBay, I never had less than 500 auctions going at a given time. Usually I had more like 1,000 individual auctions going at once. Some things didn't sell, that's OK, though, they just got re-listed again. Most items, though, sold well, and resold again and again, for years on end.

The next key in being able to do this kind of auction volume is to automate as much of the process as you can. When I was doing eBay, almost every step of the auction process was automated, meaning that computers did most of the work, I did very little. In reality, what I did was mostly just reply to e-mails that came from buyers and potential buyers of my auctions.

How can you automate all of this? Use an auction automation service. I doubt that there are any big sellers (Power Sellers) on eBay who run things manually. They all use some service to automate the process. When I was doing eBay, I used a service called AuctionWorks, later renamed to MarketWorks, and now having been purchased by ChannelAdvisor. With MarketWorks, everything was automated. Items were relisted for auction automatically, feedback was posted automatically for my customers, e-mails were sent to customers to let them know whenever anything was happening. If I marked that an item had been shipped, an e-mail was sent to the customer to let them know! If there was a tracking number for the shipping, that was included in the e-mail.

Of course, on all of those e-mails, I wrote them myself the first time, so that they were written in the language the way that I use it. But, after writing the e-mails one time, the software did the rest, just filling in the appropriate fields and such.

Without using a service like MarketWorks, you will never be able to get the most out of eBay selling, you simply won't have the time. I know that before I started using such a service, I found it a full time endeavor running 5 or 6 auctions at a time. With MarketWorks, I had no problem with 500 auctions all running at a single time!

So, my first suggestion as a way to earn money without getting a job is to start selling on eBay, and also other online auction services. There are, after all, other online auctions popping up every day, so try them out too. However, in today's marketplace, eBay is the 800 pound gorilla, so most of your sales will certainly be through eBay if you go into the online auction business.

I know right away that the first question that you have is "what do I sell?" Well, that is for you to decide. Maybe something that you make yourself. Maybe some local handicraft type items. T-shirts, caps and such? How about food items that people abroad might want, and can buy them from you? The ideas are unlimited, it is up to you to find the right items, though!

# 2 – EBAY SELLING SERVICE

I mentioned in the previous chapter that selling on eBay might be a good way to earn money from anywhere in the world. Well, I have another business idea that would put you selling on eBay, but not having to constantly find things to sell!

What I am talking about now is that you would open up a storefront in your local area where you would accept items from people and sell them on eBay. Let's say that a lady has an antique watch that she wants to sell, but she has no idea how to do it. You could take the watch in, and sell it on eBay for her. For example, you would charge her a flat price for listing the item for her, plus a percentage of the selling price.

There are stores in the USA like this that have popped up over the years, and many of them are very successful. I see no reason why such a store where I live in the Philippines could not also prove to be a good business. It could really be done in any country. As a matter of fact, I believe that it might be an even better business here than in the States. Why? Because I believe that many of the items that people would bring in to sell here would be more unique than what people in the States have and offer for sale. For example, items like jewelry and such that you can buy here have a different style, a different look compared to what you see in the States. Because such items would be more "unique" on eBay, I feel that they would have little competition, and thus could be more popular and sell better, sort of a fresh look, if you know what I mean.

# 3 – AMAZON FBA

## FBA - Fulfillment by Amazon

There is a relatively new program which I am VERY excited about. This is a program being offered by Amazon, and I believe that you can make a ton of money doing it. The program that I am talking about is called Fulfillment by Amazon, or FBA.

I first heard about FBA on a Podcast that I was listening to in March 2014. When I heard of it, I was amazed and intrigued. I knew instantly that it was something that was for me. I wanted to get involved without a doubt.

Under the FBA program, you will acquire goods, ship them to Amazon and Amazon will sell the items and fulfill the orders. So, your end of the work is to find items that will sell on Amazon, prepare your inventory based on Amazon's easy to follow instructions, ship your items to Amazon, and then spend the money that you make!

I have yet to use FBA, but I have done a lot of research into the system, and I know enough people using FBA to know that it is a winner.

On the podcast where I originally learned about FBA, there was a couple being interviewed who had been doing FBA for some months already. While they were still relatively young in the business, they were making a profit of around $100,000 (US Dollars) per month. That's pretty amazing.

The process that this couple described in their interview was relatively simple.

Firstly, there are apps available for Smartphones and iPhones that will scan barcodes on products, then look the items up on Amazon to see how much Amazon was selling the item for, how fast it is selling, etc. The couple has one of these apps on their phone.

So, one or two days per week, the couple goes to stores around their area. Places like Target or Walmart. Any stores where you can find closeout items, discounted items and such would be a perfect target for this activity. So, this couple would go from one store to another and just look around to see what items might be on sale with a good deal. They would particularly concentrate on special aisles in the stores that had been set up for clearing out goods that had been discontinued from inventory. When they find these clearance aisles, they will just scan each and every item on clearance and see if it is a good deal. As an example, they found some kind of special sponges on clearance at Target and scanned them. The sponges were being sold at Target for a low price, something like $2.00 or so. When they checked Amazon, they found that the sponges were around $20, or ten times the price they could be purchased for at Target! They proceeded to purchase every sponge available at Target, and also traveled to about a half dozen other Target stores in the area to purchase all of the stock available at each location. The sponge was just one item purchased, and there were many other items purchased on that same trip which would later be sold on Amazon using FBA. The couple did this every week, and spend thousands of dollars each week buying inventory for later sale on Amazon.

Now, buying the product is not the whole job, in fact it is only the first step. After acquiring the product, you must make sure it is in "new" condition for it to be sold on Amazon. If the packages are soiled or damaged, you cannot sell them on Amazon. You will need to clean up the packages if necessary and if possible. If it is not possible to make the package in "like new" condition you cannot sell it on Amazon. You must label the packages based on Amazon's guidelines. In fact, Amazon will give you full instructions on what must be done to make each item acceptable, and where to ship the merchandise. It is likely that you will have to make numerous shipments of product, so that there will be stock available in all, or many of Amazon's warehouses.

Once your products have been purchased, processed and shipped out, your part of the job is done for the most part. Amazon does the selling and the shipping, your next job on those items will be to get the money from Amazon. Of course, your other job will be to get out and search for more items that you can sell through Amazon.

## FBA for Expats

This whole FBA program sounds great! But, it is not perfect for expats. Why? Because shipping mass product to Amazon would be quite expensive if you are shipping from overseas. Shipping from overseas and having to compete against people who are using local shipping to send the same products to Amazon's warehouses could make it impossible to compete for an expat.

There are, however, still ways to make FBA work for an expat, in my view. Let's have a look at those possible solutions.

## Unique Products

Living abroad gives you the opportunity to find products that are not available in the USA. There are lots of products that you can find in countries all over the world that the American consumer has never seen before. You can take advantage of these products to get a "unique factor" on Amazon FBA. You could possibly be the first person to offer a certain product on Amazon, but you have to do your research. If hundreds of other sellers are already offering the item, it may not be worth your effort and expense to ship the items to the United States.

However, if you can find products that are not available on Amazon currently, you really could hit the jackpot on FBA. There are two things to look for. Firstly, look for products that are unique to the country where you are living, but would be wanted by American consumers. There are many products like that out there, if you just do the research to find the items. Secondly, you can take advantage of the huge number of immigrants in the United States. For example, where I live in the Philippines, there are millions of Filipinos who have immigrated to the USA. There are some uniquely Filipino products that are not widely available in the USA. But, those millions of Filipinos would love to get their hands on these items. Perhaps the average American consumer would have no interest in the product, but the Filipinos in the USA would love to get these items. Because of this, if I can acquire these products in the Philippines at a good price, if you can purchase in large quantities and ship the items by container load to the USA, to Amazon, and then sell through FBA. This is very possible to do. Now, if you do that, though, you will need to invest a significant amount of money in the cost of the goods (in container quantity), and also the shipping costs. But, given the large quantity of items, the per unit shipping cost would be minimal.

**Small Sized Products**

If you find an item in your country of residence which is small in size and light in weight, and you think that the item would be in demand in the States, you may have just found the perfect item for FBA. This is because an item that is small and light can generally be shipped inexpensively. If you can ship at a low cost, you really don't need to buy in huge quantity to keep the per unit shipping cost low. You could buy in a smaller "test quantity" to see how the item does in the US market by selling on FBA.

**Partner with somebody in the USA**

Another alternative would be to see if you could find a partner in the USA. This could be a person who also wants to make some extra money. This person would need to be able to take care of product acquisition and shipping to Amazon. Now, as I described the process, this is the majority of the work, so you will need to find a place where you can fit into the process to justify your share of the profits. What I would suggest is to see if you can find a person who is not very computer savvy, somebody that would have a hard time dealing with the online part of the business. With a person like this, you could handle the computer end of the business and let the other person handle the physical part of it that would need the person to be in the USA.

So, as you see, there are certainly ways that FBA can be put to use by an expat. You will still be at a competitive disadvantage against FBA sellers based in the USA, but I do expect that the FBA platform will continue to evolve, and that it will evolve in ways that will be beneficial to expats. What I do know is that this is a fantastic opportunity for somebody who lives the expat life to make money, and I believe it is important to explore this platform and look for ways that it could be put to use in your situation.

# 4 – AMAZON FBA SUPPORT BUSINESS

As I noted in the previous chapter, Amazon has a relatively new program called FBA, or Fulfillment by Amazon. Under the program, you ship products to Amazon and Amazon sells your products on their website.

Now, in my opinion, this is all very easy. Amazon gives you instructions on where to send your products, how to ship it, how to package, labeling of the products, etc. Compared to selling items via ecommerce even 5 or 6 years ago, this opens some fantastic possibilities for you and for me too! Now, if you compare this program with the times when I first started doing business on the Internet, back 25 years ago, well, we are talking night and day.

So, the opportunity is fantastic. But, there is a downside too. If you are not living in the USA, it can be difficult. How? Why? Because if you have products that are in the USA, but you are located in, for example, the Philippines, like me, it can be difficult to meet Amazon's stringent shipping and packaging requirements. You are not there to do the shipping and packaging, so you have to figure out how to meet the standards without being present to be able to monitor it yourself.

There is a solution that I thought of, though. And, doing a bit of Googling I have found that the solution that I came up with is in play, but only to a very small extent.

My idea is that people who are very familiar with Amazon FBA can start a Fulfillment Center of their own where people could ship their FBA products to, and then this Fulfillment Center would prepare the items to meet Amazon's standards and then ship the products to Amazon. So, if you had such a business, you would be a middle man to fulfill the needs for the seller and get the product to Amazon, for a price of course. You would be fulfilling the needs of the FBA seller.

The way I see it, there are two different types of people who would use such a service. Firstly, people like me who live outside the USA. Secondly, people who are "low-tech" and don't know how to do all of the things that Amazon requires. There are a lot of these kind of people who are scared to learn new things, or just don't have the time.

So, in my searching, I found only one such business in the USA, it is in Wisconsin. I also found one such place in Europe, in Denmark. Others may exist, but these were the only ones that I could find.

In looking over the website of the company in Wisconsin, I can see a number of advantages of using them, or similar companies if they exist. On the site, they specifically point out the benefits that they offer for International Sellers. One example is that if you ship goods from your overseas location, there is a good possibility that some items may be damaged or broken during shipping. The center will check your items and remove any items that were damaged. If you send too much damaged merchandise directly to Amazon, they may ban your account, or at the very least you will receive negative feedback from customers who buy and receive the damaged goods. Getting negative feedback from customers could really kill off your business. Basically, the flow of the system offered by this company would include:

- Receiving your merchandise shipment

- Inspecting the goods for any damage

- Removing any price tags from the packaging, as required by Amazon

- Create labels with SKU numbers as required by Amazon's FBA program

- Shrink wrap, Bubble wrap, and bundle your items for shipment

- Box, label and generally prepare your shipment per Amazon guidelines, using an approved shipping partner

If you will be receiving multiple shipments of a product, the fulfillment center will store your items until all of your shipments have arrived, so that you can take advantage of shipping your entire shipment in bulk to receive better freight prices.

This fulfillment center will take care of every single thing you need to be able to get done to sell through FBA, even if you are not on the scene.

OK, so some of you are wondering how this will help you. You are in the USA and you are willing to do everything needed to sell via FBA. Yes, no problem, but what I am saying is that you can start your own fulfillment center and have customers from all over the world who will use your services so that they can sell on FBA. Many Americans don't realize that there are people all over the world who desire to be part of this kind of program that gives them access to the huge market of American consumers! It is a wonderful opportunity for you.

What I would recommend is that you sell on FBA yourself for a while. By doing that, you will learn the system, understand what Amazon is looking for, learn the right way of doing things. Once you know that, you can tap a huge market of people who cannot easily work with FBA due to their location, or inability to understand or even learn the Amazon requirements. You will be able to make money from FBA without even selling anything yourself! Of course you can make even more if you take care of your own orders and also the merchandise of other Amazon sellers who need your services!

I really believe that FBA is a great system to make a good income, and now I have shown you that you can actually make money through FBA in different ways that the conventional. Give it some thought, and you will likely come up with other types of FBA revenue streams as well.

# 5 – DS DOMINATION

In the recent past, a "system" has come into place called DS Domination. At the same time, I both think that it is a great thing, and I also think that it is something to stay away from. How can I think both things simultaneously? Well, read on and you will see.

DS Domination perfected a strategy where you sell on eBay, but your source your products from Amazon. I know that this sounds strange, but that is what people using DS Domination are doing, and they are making a lot of money doing it.

What these folks are doing, basically, is finding items in Amazon's inventory which they can sell for a higher price on eBay. In other words, if Amazon is selling an item for $20, it is possible for you to sell it on eBay for, say, $30 and make a profit. The profit would not be $10 on that example transaction, because there are eBay fees and such to consider, but maybe you would make $8 or something in that area.

So, you find those items on Amazon that you think you can sell at a higher price, and you list the items on eBay. I know, I know… it doesn't make sense that if a product is available on Amazon for $20 somebody would pay you $30 for the item. But, it happens. I promise you that. When I first started hearing about DS Domination from friends, I thought the same thing…

Why would somebody pay me more when they can get it on Amazon for less?

Well, they do. I don't know why, I suppose that it is just because the nature of people is that they don't always shop around and look for deals. I have a friend who is involved in DS Domination, and he does fairly well with it, although he is more or less just a beginner. I would say that he has been using the system for less than 6 months, but earning good money already. A few months back, I talked with him via Skype, and we also had his DS Domination mentor on the call as well. My friend's name is Dave, and his mentor is Ron. They told me all about DS Domination. I think their main goal was to recruit me to join DS Domination, although I am thankful that they did not use a hard sell technique to draw me in. They simply told me of the program and its benefits. I asked a lot of questions and learned a lot about the program.

One of the points that I kept asking about was that question… why would people buy from me when they can buy from Amazon for less? I can see two reasons why it would be better to buy from Amazon:

Firstly, the price is lower for the exact same item, so it's a no-brainer.

Secondly, Amazon is a large trusted vendor, while I am just an unknown person, so the trust would be there for Amazon, but not for me.

Well, whatever the reason may be, Dave and Ron showed me proof of their sales, and compared what they were selling to what Amazon was selling, and it is exact. Of course it is exact, because they are getting the products from Amazon to begin with!

Now, as I have explained it so far, it is a beautiful program. It works like a charm, and is very easy. But, there are some things that I have yet to tell you about, things which make it even more of a winner, especially for expats and other people who do not live in the USA.

Believe it or not, Dave, Ron and the thousands of others using DS Domination do not buy anything from Amazon for selling. They simply sell the Amazon items, then if somebody buys from them, they go to Amazon and buy the item, and let Amazon ship it to the person that they sold to on eBay! Yep, that's correct, they never even have to touch the product. They are, in fact, using Amazon as a drop shipper. In other words, they sell the product, then have Amazon ship it directly to the person that bought it instead of to them.

In all of my time of doing ecommerce, I have always been against using a drop shipper. I don't like to do that because I am putting my personal reputation as a seller in the hands of the drop shipper. If the item is not shipped on time, or if it is not shipped at all, that will damage my reputation. However, when the drop shipper is Amazon, I really don't have a problem putting my reputation in their hands. Why? Because Amazon is very conscientious about shipping on time, quality goods. They are not a shady company, in fact quite the opposite. So, I trust that if I order from Amazon and have it shipped to Mr. Joe Buyer, I am certain that it will get to him on time.

Now, the way that my friends were doing things, as I said, was to go buy the goods on Amazon and have it shipped to the person who made the purchase on eBay. What they are doing, to be more specific, is using the option on Amazon to ship the item as a gift. If you ship it as a gift, the person it is shipped to does not get an invoice showing the price you paid and such, so that keeps it your secret. Now, I know that you are thinking that the person who bought it could go on the Amazon website and see how much was paid for the item on Amazon. That is true, but I am told that it rarely ever creates a problem. If your buyer insists on making a problem out of it, you can always refund them the difference in price, but that is very rare.

## A note on shipping

Amazon offers a program called Amazon Prime, where you pay an amount (at the time of writing it is $99 per year) to be a member. If you are a member of Amazon Prime, you get free shipping. Everything you purchase on Amazon will be shipped to you for free if you are an Amazon Prime member.

Some people doing DS Domination use Amazon Prime free shipping for shipping their DS Domination purchases that are shipped to their eBay customers. However, it is my understanding that the terms of service for Amazon Prime allow you to only get free shipping on items for your personal use, not for commercial goods - items that you are selling to others. So, if you try to use Amazon Prime for shipping your commercial shipments, you should be cautious and understand that you may lose your Amazon Prime privileges for doing so.

## My take on DS Domination

I feel that DS Domination is a super strategy. It is something that really makes life easy for an expat who lives overseas to get involved in the ecommerce game. ecommerce is a huge business, but the biggest market is the USA, so being outside the USA is a huge disadvantage.

I have said that eBay levels the playing field between little guys like you and I vs. the big businesses. Well, DS Domination levels the playing field between those of us who live overseas vs. those who live in the USA and want to sell via ecommerce. It is that simple.

But, there is a downside to DS Domination. In my opinion, DS Domination is an MLM or Pyramid scheme. At the time of this writing, DS Domination charges $20 per month to join the program and get all the benefits that are offered to those who are members. In addition to using the system for selling on eBay (and other marketplaces) as a member you can also recruit others to join, and you will then get a percentage of the membership fees that they pay. Additionally, as your recruits get others to join, you will get a cut on all of the other new members that are recruited in your chain. Getting a cut of more money is a good thing, of course, but let's be honest... this is a classic Pyramid setup, something that usually doesn't last forever, and ends up crashing. But, the good thing is that it offers other benefits, not just getting money for recruiting people.

Notice that I am not recruiting you in this book. I am not giving you links on where to sign up. I am not going to make anything if you sign up. Why? Because I am not a member of DS Domination. I have studied it and elected not to join, although I came very close to doing so. Since the monthly fee is only $20, I don't feel that it is evil or a huge rip-off. I feel that there is actually a fair amount of value in joining, especially if you will be new at selling on eBay.

For me, though, because I have a great deal of experience in selling on eBay, I do not feel that there are huge benefits to joining DS Domination. I have been told by people trying to recruit me that I should not sell on eBay without using DS Domination because I might break some eBay rules and thus get my account banned from selling on eBay. They told me that DS Domination would save me from such a fate. For somebody who is new at selling on eBay this may be a fact. But, with my experience, and having gone many years of selling on eBay without ever having a problem with having my account banned or any other such thing, I am confident that I could sell on eBay while using Amazon as my fulfillment partner without running afoul of the eBay rules.

If you are new, though, I don't think that joining DS Domination is going to hurt you, in fact I think it will help you. Perhaps it will help you even more than I think it will. But, if you are just getting started and need direction, I feel that $20 per month is cheap, and I am certain that if you work the system you will make a lot more than the $20 that it will cost you to join DS Domination. So, for beginners, I will recommend DS Domination. For experienced eBay sellers, I don't think it is necessary.

If you want to join DS Domination, just do a search on Google or any of the search engines, it will be easy to find where to join.

# 6 - DVD AND CD PRODUCTION

Recently, I started offering products on CD and DVD disks. I am using eBay and Amazon FBA to sell these informational disks.

Basically, what I am doing is that I create things like online courses on websites, and I sell memberships for people to take the course online. When the online course is completely ready for selling, I will then also put the course on DVD (or CD if it is small enough in size, but I almost always publish on DVD). Once you already have the course created, it is relatively easy to port the content over to a DVD disk.

Once I have the DVD disk created, I then use a US company called "Kunaki" (www.kunaki.com) to make and publish the DVDs for me. Kunaki is set up where you upload the DVD (or CD) content as a "product". Then, anytime you sell the product, you just go to their website and click how many of that particular product you wish to make and have shipped.

So, for example, if I list the particular online course on eBay, and it sells, I just go to Kunaki, have the DVD produced and shipped directly to my eBay customer. The same holds true for Amazon FBA selling. If I set up an FBA shipment on Amazon, and Amazon gives me the instructions on where to ship the DVDs, I just go to Kunaki and have the DVDs made and shipped per Amazon's instructions. Amazon will usually have you split the order into 2 or 3 different shipments, going to warehouses in different parts of the USA. In this case, all you do is order 3 different shipments at Kunaki, per the instructions that Amazon gives you. It is very easy and also quite quick. Shipments from Kunaki are from Nevada, so if Amazon has me ship to California or Arizona warehouses, it usually takes only about 2 days for the shipment to arrive. East Coast shipments generally arrive at Amazon in a week or so.

Nothing is cooler than developing your own product, having it manufactured for you and shipping to Amazon. When you see your product listed on the Amazon website, it is a real good feeling! The feeling is even better when the product starts selling, and when Amazon starts depositing the money into your bank account!

One downside of selling products on Amazon using FBA is that if a whole bunch of FBA sellers all start selling the same product, unless you are willing to cut the price, you won't get the sales (the person selling at the lowest price gets the sales). But, when you develop your own product that nobody else has access to, there is no way that you can have competition! You get all of the sales, because you are actually the manufacturer as well as a seller! It doesn't get better than that.

The truth is, this chapter is about using Kunaki to make DVD and CD disks for you, it is not about eBay or FBA. I mention eBay and FBA only as a suggestion on how to sell the products that you are having manufactured by Kunaki. However, there is no limit to how you can sell those DVD products! You are only limited by your own imagination! Maybe you would want to sell at flea markets, garage sales, through your own website. How about selling through your online mailing and newsletter lists? There really is no limit to the selling possibilities.

Know what the really great news is on using Kunaki to do disk manufacturing? The price of the finished product is just $1 per disk plus shipping charges. Kunaki is a bit expensive on shipping, but when you balance out the shipping with the cost of the DVD, you will find that it is all very cheap. Usually, a disk can be sent out worldwide for $4.30 shipping charge. So, the overall cost is $1 for the disk and $4.30 shipping for a total cost of $5.30 per DVD. If you are ordering in larger quantities (more than 1 disk per shipment) then the cost is even lower. Check the Kunaki website for current costs.

Think about this, though.. at the highest, the cost is $5.30 to have a single disk sent to a customer or to Amazon. I have many DVD based products on Amazon that I sell for $149 (and other prices). The cost of the item is $5 or so, and I sell for $149. That is a pretty nice markup! Now, Amazon gets a share for selling, there are various fees and such. But, whenever I sell one of those $149 courses, I get about $122 or so. It costs me $5.30 or less for everything including shipping, and I get $122. It is hard to go wrong with those numbers.

Another great thing is that these are not cheap CDR disks for DVDR. These disks look just like CDs or DVDs that you buy in the store. The disk and the case are professionally printed with graphics that you create yourself and upload. Glossy finish, professional just like any retail disks that you might be buying. The customers will not be able to tell that you are just an individual guy living in Panama or the Philippines, or anywhere else in the world. When the open the package from Amazon, they won't be able to tell if you are Sony or some other big media company, or just a guy cranking out a living in the jungle somewhere, the quality is that good!

If you have ideas for any kind of product that you can sell on CD or DVD - if you are a musician and want to sell your own music, or if you are a software developer who wants to take advantage of large marketplaces in the USA, well, Kunaki is the perfect solution for you in my view.

I highly recommend Kunaki. They have done wonders for my sales and earnings, and I am sure they will do great for you as well.

# SECTION 2 - BLOGGING

Ways to make money that are related to blogging.

# 7 - BLOGGING

More specifically Professional Blogging. Did you know that there is actually big money to be made from Blogging? I first learned about blogging as a money making enterprise in 2004. It intrigued me, and I spent a lot of time studying it.

I first learned about blogging to earn money by reading a blog called "ProBlogger" (http://www.ProBlogger.net) by Darren Rowse, who lives in Australia. At the time, Darren had just broken out into earning big money through his blogging efforts by getting a check from Google AdSense for around $13,000 for a single month, as my memory serves me. For Darren, this was just a start, he has gone on to earn much more than that, and you really should read his site to get all the scoop on how he does it. There is no doubt that Darren has put together an impressive business through his blogging, and his hard work has paid off big time.

I, myself, decided to try to earn money through blogging after seeing what Darren had accomplished. I quickly learned one thing, though, it is not easy, and it is not automatic that you will make big amounts of money. Currently, I have built up my various blogs to where I am earning in the area of about $7,000 per month from Blogging. It takes work, though. You must provide quality content in order to attract enough readers to bring in that kind of money. It is my hope that I can increase that amount by a multiple in coming years, but nothing is certain. However, as I have followed other well-known bloggers, as they have managed to reach a similar level of income, things took off and the number grew exponentially, and I want to make that happen for myself too. You can do that too, if you are willing to try hard enough. Remember, I already said, you have to work, nothing comes free!

The thing is, I feel, through my experience, with a minimal amount of work, you indeed can get up to earning $1,000 or so per month.

How do you earn money blogging? Well, there are actually many ways to earn money through blogging. The most common way is to earn money through Google AdSense. With AdSense, Google will place advertisements on your blog, which are contextual (they are targeted to your audience, based on the content on your site). When your readers click on these ads, you get paid. Google pays once per month, at the end of the month. Payments are held back by one month. In other words, the money that you earn in February is paid at the end of March, and so on. Another catch is that you won't be paid anything until you earn $100. Any month that you are owed

$100 or more, you will be paid. If you earn less than $100, the money will be held in your account until the balance gets up to $100 or more. For me, I have not had a problem with this, as I have never earned less than $100 in any colander month. Others can take months to reach this threshold, though.

Google is not your only choice, though! There are other advertising companies that will also work with you to place advertisements on your site. Another Advertising Agency to consider is Chitika. The number of such advertisers is in the dozen or more now, although there are only a handful of big players in the game. My biggest earners are Google AdSense, Chitika and Text Link Ads, in that order.

Darren, the ProBlogger, constantly drives home the point that there is more than one way to earn money by blogging. You can earn money from your blog by placing ads, as I have described. The other way to is to earn money because of your blog, rather than directly from your blog. Feyma and I also earn money because of our blogs too. How? Well, Feyma is involved with promoting Real Estate around Davao (the city where we live), and we advertise the service on our various blogs. It has been quite successful, and it works because those who enjoy reading our blogs are her customers. This income, because of our blogs, is one of our best income source related to blogging at this time.

Really, since I originally wrote about using advertising to earn money from you blog, back in 2007 or 2008, I feel that the amount of money that you will make from advertising (Google or other partners) has shrunk significantly. In fact, I have come to the point where I run only a very minimal number of ad placements on my site. I still run ads, but mostly advertisements for my own products. I have things like eBooks, services like consulting, a private investigative service, a language course and such that I produce myself, and I advertise those services and products to my blog readers. The nice thing about such products is that instead of earning a small advertising fee, I earn the entire revenue produced by the product sold. I have found it a much more rewarding way to go compared to running things like Google advertisements.

So, if you want to make money from blogging, how do you do it? First, choose the right topic to blog about. If you set up a very general personal blog where you talk about what kind of shampoo you bought, or what you ate for breakfast, and everything in between, you probably are not going to earn much money. You need to find a niche, target it, and write about that topic every day. If you write one post today, and another next month, or you write three this week, then it's six months before your next post, forget about it. You will never build up the audience that you need to be financially successful at blogging. Also, when you start writing every day, don't expect that you will start raking in the money that very month. It might take 6 months, even a year before you build up your audience! But, it will happen, if you are willing to spend the time and be persistent.

As a matter of fact, I recommend that you forget about putting ads on your blog at first. Just concentrate on providing interesting content for people to read. Go around to other blogs and place comments there. When people find that you have valuable things to say in your comments, they will go check out your blog! If you just leave a comment that says "go visit my blog" people will ignore it, and consider you to basically be a spammer. Leave information that is valuable on blogs that are related in subject to yours. People will come over and check your blog out! That being said, don't go around and leave all these comments until you have some content on your site! If your blog has only one post, and that post says "Hello Everybody" - when people go there, they won't come back, because there is nothing of value to read!

Now, what about where to blog? There are plenty of blogging services where you can set up a free blog. I don't recommend using those places. If you are going to be a Professional Blogger, act like a pro! Set up your own website, with your own blogging software (I recommend Wordpress.org for the software). Don't go the free route, you'll regret it later. After all, for $13 per year for the domain name, and a few dollars per month, you can have your own site.

Blogging can pay off. I know that, because I am doing it, and I make money by blogging. You can too. Just be patient, don't be afraid to work, and hang in there! Persistence pays off. If you quit after a week or a month, you can forget about ever being successful with it!

I have mentioned a number of times in this section that blogging takes time to build up. You have to blog regularly over a longer period of time to build a regular audience. However, the good thing you will find is that once you start building up that regular audience, you can then start other, new blogs and websites, and it is much easier to get started, because your regular audience on one of your blogs will often follow you over to your new sites. So, that early grind of blogging daily will pay off big for you if you do it and keep doing it!

# 8 – PAID BLOGGING

Back toward the beginning of this book, I told you how you could set up a blog and place ads and such on your blog to make money. While I really believe that is a great way to earn a living, there is also another way that you can earn money by blogging.

Did you know that there are actually companies that will pay you to blog? It's true! Now, you must blog about the topic that they tell you to blog about, and you must put links into your post to sites where they direct you to link to, but if you follow their guidelines, they will pay you to write a post on your blog! A former employee of mine is doing this now and has told me that she is earning upward of $3,000 per month doing it! That's a nice income, or at least a nice supplement to your income.

While it is possible to make the kind of money that my ex-employee is making, I don't feel that the average person will be able to generate that kind of money doing paid blogging. Making an income of say $500 to $1,000 per month would not be hard to do with this method, I believe, that is not "job replacing" money, it is more of just a supplement. Still, though, if you need the money, $500 or more is nothing to pass by.

Here is a list of companies that I recommend if you are interested in doing this:

Smorty/Write.inc

Pay Per Post

Payu2Blog

ReviewMe

Blogvertise

Blogitive

Each of these companies pay for you to post on your blog, as I have explained.

**Here is how it works:**

You join the network by going to their website and signing up. They will review your blog to make sure that it meets their standards, and if they approve your blog, you are then taken in as a member of the service. Then, anytime that you want to blog for payment, you just go log into the site of the service that you are using and you will find a list of "Opps" or Opportunities. They will list all of the opportunities that you qualify for, which is determined by the ranking of your blog. Each opportunity is simply an offer of a certain amount of money for posting one single post on your blog. Each Opp offered will pay between $3.50 up to $500.00 for a single blog post. The better your blog is rated, the higher amount of payment you are eligible for. Each blog post must be from 50 up to 500 words, depending on the requirements of the company that is making the offer. Each opp that is given will list the specifics of what is required to make the blog post eligible for the payment. If you follow the requirements, no problem, you will be paid on a regular schedule.

My former employee tells me that now that she has been doing this for almost a year now, she even gets offers directly from companies who want her to post the blogs. She says that these are paid instantly to her PayPal account in most cases.

Blogging on a Pay Per Post basis like this can be quite lucrative, and more of a direct payment, almost like working for an employer, compared to sort of being self-employed by putting up ads and such on your blog, as I described early.

In order to get started in this, I recommend that you start up a blog of your own, get it going by posting for a few months and establishing your site with some credibility and page rank, then registering for the services so that you can start making money.

# 9 – BLOG SUPPORT BUSINESS

There are actually a few different things that you can do to service bloggers worldwide. As you can imagine, there are millions of people around the world who are Blogging these days, so if you can only get a tiny share of the market, you can make good money by offering Blog support services.

What kind of services am I talking about? Well, What I am talking about are things like these:

- Offer to set up blogs for people who don't know how to set up their own blog. Of course, you will charge a price for the setup!

- Hire a team of people who can write, and hire them out as commenters or even ghost writers of blog content. Clients can then hire you to have your employees post comments on their blogs to kind of "get things going."

- Have people who can troubleshoot different blog platforms for clients.

- Have people who can take care of administrative tasks for customers.

- Keep people's blogs current. Software updates need to be done, both core WordPress software and also plugins.

As you can see, there are lots of different things that you can do for bloggers that many would be willing to pay you for.

Most bloggers will not pay for these kind of services, but in my opinion, your target customers come from two groups:

A-List bloggers, i.e. big bloggers. These people have such a huge job to do in keeping up with their various blogs that you can certainly attract them by taking on some of the more mundane aspects of running a blog. If your staff is competent, you can certainly help somebody who is on the "A List."

People who want to blog, but are basically computer-illiterate. There are a lot of people who are interested in the Internet, but they basically know very little when it comes to technical information. Figuring out how to install a blog is way beyond what they can figure out. This kind of person is a perfect target customer. You can make money in several ways from this person –

firstly the installation of the blog itself. Secondly, by installing things like plugins for the blog and other enhancements to improve their blog. Thirdly, you can also offer training courses on how to blog. Where to enter the text, how to put a picture into the blog post, etc. These are all relatively simple things that a lot of people are totally mystified by. You can even put together some videos on how to do these things (by using screen casting technology), and sell the videos.

There is a huge market of people who want to learn how to blog, take advantage of it by offering training for those who want to learn.

There are also plenty of people who are over-burdened with menial tasks who would gladly outsource it to a place where labor is relatively inexpensive. You are the guy in the middle who knows both sides and can solve the problems!

I have personally taken this "blog support" to a whole new level by starting my own company called "CurvePress" where I offer a suite of WordPress services. Everything from website design and construction to site maintenance to WordPress training. I have many avenues for earning through CurvePress, and also offer excellent and valuable services to my clients. You can do it too, it is a large market of potential customers.

# 10 – FREE BLOGGING SERVICE

Unless you have been hiding under a rock for the past 15 years or so, you have undoubtedly heard about Blogging! Blogging is the practice where people set up websites where they record regular posts about whatever topic they choose. Some people blog about their day to day life. Others blog about Global Warming, still others blog about Animals, or whatever topic interests them.

The vast majority of people who blog do so on a free blogging site. Such sites would include:

- Wordpress.com

- Blogger.com

- and many others

Here's a little secret that you might not know... you can set up such a service yourself, and it is actually fairly simple to do.

"But, Bob..." you say, "those are free services! How can I make money on that?"

Well, my friend, actually you can make money quite simply. You see, on such a service, YOU control the templates that can be used by the bloggers. You can insert advertising onto the template that pays YOU, not the blogger.

How do you set this up? My recommendation would be to use WordPress MU (Multi-User). WordPress MU is the software that is being used by Wordpress.com and some of the other services as well. It is a WordPress platform that will accept multiple users. You can literally set up hundreds of thousands of blogs on a single WordPress installation. Everybody who wants to have a blog can have one, using your single installation of WordPress MU. It's that simple.

WordPress MU is free Open-Source software. Anybody can use it free of charge.

With WordPress MU, you get to choose what templates are available for the bloggers to use. When you prepare the templates, you can insert advertising (Google AdSense, Affiliate ads, whatever) right into the template. The user has no choice but to show the ads, since they are built right into the template.

Now, if you only attract a few bloggers, you might not make much. But, if you make your blogging site really attractive and attract thousands of bloggers, you could make a fortune. For example, let's say that you, after establishing yourself, have 5,000 bloggers using your site. If each of these bloggers averages just 10 cents per day in ad revenue, you would be making $500 per day from the advertising. The cost of maintaining the service is quite small, actually less than $500 per month (unless you need to hire employees, which I do not believe will be needed). Imagine, if you had 100,000 bloggers using your site? The income potential is outstanding!

# SECTION 3 - ON THE WEB

Strictly web-based ways to make money.

# 11 – E-COMMERCE

While things like eBay could be considered as e-commerce, what I am talking about here is more of doing it on your own. Not using somebody else's marketplace to sell things, but to start your own market or store on the Internet. Of all the businesses that I have been involved in while living in the Philippines, e-Commerce has been the best to me in terms of providing me an income. Now, when I start talking about putting up a store on the Internet, I know that many readers will start thinking to themselves that the cost of opening their own store is sky high. I mean, inventory of goods and such can lead to a lot of money. Well, that is true, buying a bunch of stock of merchandise is not cheap! However, keep in mind that we are talking about an electronic store, and I have not said anything about buying any inventory! For the most part, I don't stock any merchandise for my online stores. When I get an order for an item, I go buy that item. Now, on a few occasions I have purchased inventory, but only rarely. The only times that I have done this, though are at times like during holidays, and when a certain piece of merchandise seemed to be in short supply. For example, during Valentine's Day, if there is a certain box of chocolates that I know will sell very well, but the store only has a limited number available, I might buy up all that they have. This way, I can assure myself of having stock to last me through the holiday without running out, and I know that the item will sell anyway. However, except in this type of situation, I never buy any inventory.

The next thing that people are thinking now is that I can't get wholesale pricing if I just go buy one or two items when I sell them. Well, that is true. Also, I really don't care! I buy retail, and I mark up my prices enough that I make a very good percentage on the items. Remember, I am talking about doing business in the Philippines, and many retail prices are unbelievably low anyway, so marking them up by a fairly large amount still keeps the items looking quite affordable to people who are my customers (I only sell to customers overseas, not within the Philippines – there are tax reasons to do that). By the time you figure in the amount that I am saving by not having my money tied up in Inventory costs, the lost savings of 20% or whatever by buying retail is virtually meaningless anyway.

Now, when I talk about e-Commerce, what exactly do I mean? Well, I mean selling merchandise on the Internet. I personally have about a half dozen e-commerce sites right now, and have had up to 15 at one time in the past. Some of those I have closed down, others have been rolled together into a single store. Of all my e-commerce sites that I've ever tried, I only had one that I closed down because it didn't do well (and that store still paid for itself, just didn't produce enough profit to get excited about). I have closed down other stores because of my lack of ability to get the product any longer, which was beyond my control.

What kind of money can you make in e-Commerce? Well, you can make a lot of money, I won't lie. My two most successful e-commerce sites are two totally different ideas, and each made a lot of money for me. Let's have a look at each of them:

## Gift Business

I actually currently have several e-commerce sites in the gift business. We sell gift items to men worldwide (except men in the Philippines), and we deliver the gifts to their girlfriends in the Philippines. In other words, a man in Australia might purchase a dozen roses from us, and we will deliver the flowers to his girlfriend in Cebu or Cagayan de Oro, Philippines. We deliver to any address in the Philippines. We sell flowers, chocolates, computers, food (like pizza, KFC chicken, etc.), groceries, jewelry and just about any other thing you can think of. We have even sold motorcycles and jeepneys in the past, although we are no longer handling those items. As I said earlier, this has been a very profitable business for me. I have actually earned more doing this business than I earned when I had a full time (good) job in the USA. This business has actually grown into multiple e-commerce shops! I have opened up more than one such shop selling the same items. Basically, I have set myself up as my own competitor, giving me more than one chance to attract customers.

## Shampoo Business

One of my businesses which no longer exists is an e-commerce site where I used to sell shampoo. Shampoo? Yes, shampoo. And, it is quite a story. You see, not long after I moved to the Philippines, one day I was walking through a grocery store, and I spotted something on the shelf that caught my attention. It was a bottle of shampoo. This bottle of shampoo was familiar to me too, although I had not seen the brand in years, decades even. The shampoo was a brand that was quite famous and popular during my childhood, in the 1970's. It was heavily advertised on TV at the time, but it disappeared from the market. I went home and started doing some research on the product, and found that it was mysteriously taken off the market in the early 80's. I also found out that there was a demand for the product to this day. As a matter of fact, I found that people were selling old bottles of the shampoo brand on eBay for very high prices, around $20 and more per bottle. Well, I could buy it in the stores here in the Philippines, because it was still being made and sold here. Apparently, the US company that made it originally had entered into a licensing agreement with a company in the Philippines to manufacture and sell the product in the Philippines. The company was still active in selling it here! So, I started buying the shampoo (and conditioner) and selling it on eBay. It did very well, and pretty soon, I started my own website to sell it, abandoning eBay altogether after I had built up enough market recognition to hold my own.

It didn't take long and a large catalog retailer in the USA contacted me, wanting to purchase the product to sell it to US customers via their catalog. They became a regular customer, buying 500 cases of the shampoo twice each month. Believe it or not, I made a 5 figure profit on each bulk sale, so it was a very good item for me. However, all things come to an end, and after a time, the original US manufacturer found out what was going on, and they actually put the squeeze on the Philippine manufacturer (the only place in the world where the shampoo was still manufactured), and put a stop to the production. So, that particular business went by the wayside, but other opportunities come along.

So, now I have given you a couple of examples of e-commerce sites that I have operated and am still operating.

What about getting the money from the customer? Well, it is not easy to get a merchant account if you live in the Philippines (a merchant account is the type of account that allows you to take credit cards). However, there are alternatives that will allow you to accept payments through Credit Card or other methods. My recommendations are to use PayPal or 2Checkout. Those will be covered further in the Appendix area of this book.

Basically, I am here to tell you, the e-commerce business is a great business to get into. You can serve customers anywhere in the world, and do it from the comfort of your own home, if that is what you choose to do.

To operate an e-commerce store you will need a website and shopping cart software. I personally use a program WordPress software with a Plugin called WP eStore to handle the shopping cart end of my site. WordPress is free, open-source software. The eStore plugin is a premium plugin for WordPress and costs $49. WordPress is very easy to use, very intuitive. The eStore plugin has a bit of a learning curve, but there are online tutorials on video that actually make it easy to learn. This combination of software is very flexible and I have found that I have been able to make it do things that I didn't think you could do with it! I am sure that with practice you can also make it a great fit for your needs.

You know, there are a lot of people on the internet writing books about how to make money, but can you believe all of those books? I am here to tell you that you cannot. Can you believe mine? Well, yes, you can, because I actually earn my living through these ideas that I am sharing with you.

Do my ideas work? You better believe it! Choose one or two that interest you and get busy. These kinds of earnings can be yours too!

# 12 – BUILD WEBSITES

There is no doubt that building websites is a good business! I mean, take a look at the statistics. The Internet is an entity that has only been publicly available for under 25 years. Yet, how many websites are there now? The most recent surveys show that there are more than 180 Million Websites! And, all of those websites have multiple pages that make up the site, resulting in more than 30 Billion web pages making up the World Wide Web. Now, think about this – somebody had to create all of those pages! Why not start a business designing and building webpages? It is really a booming business these days, and estimates are that it will only grow in the future, as more and more businesses and individuals get on the Web.

You don't know how to make a webpage, you say? Well, no problem. You need to hire a staff of designers and coders here in the Philippines or in some other low-cost-labor part of the world. Your job is to supervise them, and to get the work assignments from foreign companies. As in a previous example, you can use sites like eLance.com to find companies bidding for work to be done. Also, promote your service and jobs will start rolling in. The talent is available here with hundreds, actually thousands of people who can do excellent work in this realm. You are the key for them, though, in that you can put your foreign contacts to work in lining up jobs for these people to do!

Yes, there is a lot of competition in this field, but there is also a lot of work available, so don't get scared away by competition. You can find plenty of work!

Now, what about the fact that you need to buy a lot of computers, equipment and such? Well, it is true that you will need such items for each of your designers, but I have a possible solution for you. Firstly, before you go out and buy equipment to get started, why not start out by renting spaces in a local Internet Cafe? For only P20 per machine per hour or so (if you are working in the Philippines, where I live), you can have your business up and running. If you find that you can make a go of the business, then it might be time to look at purchasing such equipment!

Even if you don't know how to build a website, you can hire a staff who does!

However, even if the business takes off, you still have options on the equipment. First, if what you have been doing has been working, no need to change! If it ain't broke, don't fix it! I mean, my suggestion has been to use Internet Cafes for P20 or so per hour, per station while you are evaluating the long term potential of the business. Even after you have decided that the business has legs, if using Internet Cafes is working well, stick with it, and save money on the equipment. A second choice would be to approach the owner of an Internet Cafe that you like. Let's say that his cafe closes up at 10pm or Midnight, and re-opens at 9am the next day. Perhaps you can swing a deal with the owner to rent the place during those closed hours and you'll have the run of the place during the night. You can have your employees work during night time, and probably get the use of the Cafe at a relatively inexpensive rate. After all, whatever you pay is just gravy for the business owner, as he has been earning nothing during those hours anyway. The third option would be to go ahead and buy the equipment that you need, rent some office space and set up shop. You've had time to evaluate the success potential for the business anyway, so you should have a good idea as to how much you can afford, and you should know that it will be successful by this point.

I suspect that your biggest problem with this kind of business is going to be turnover of your employees. These type of workers will be a highly migrant lot in my opinion, so you will want to be constantly keeping an eye out for additional employees. Also, it will be important to limit the contact that your employees have with your customers, or even their knowledge of who the customers are, otherwise they may try to undercut your pricing and steal your customers. So, watch out for this.

Remember, you don't need to know how to build a website to do this! Simply hire it out, and then evaluate the finished work. If something shows up that you don't approve of, have the employee change it! It's that simple.

If you do good quality work, you will find that it is not difficult to find clients. Do a great job for a client and word of mouth will spread more quickly than you can believe!

How much should you charge for a website? Well, it depends on you. I would recommend starting out with a lower price so that you can get experience and pick up some regular clients. A low price and good quality work tends to draw plenty of takers! Over time, as you gain more experience you will also grow a larger customer base.

When your customer base grows you can do one, or both, of two things:

1. Hire more people to work for you to give you greater capacity to make more websites.

2. Raise your prices. The more you raise your price, the fewer clients you will keep or gain. So, raise your prices on a regular basis until you get to having steady work from a good number of clients, just enough to keep you busy. That balance between a higher price and the right number of clients is the equilibrium that will maximize your use of time as well as the most profit that you can make without need to expand further.

From my experience, website design is something that will make you great money. Since the first edition of this book, my income from web design and construction has gotten larger and larger. I have learned more, gotten much more expertise in the field, and gained some excellent and very regular clients. It is a business that I highly recommend.

# 13 – ASK THE EXPERT

We all have expertise on something. I mean whether it is how to raise livestock, or how to build airplanes, all of us have some kind of expertise, based on the jobs that we have done and our life experiences. Think about what areas of expertise you have, and use it to make money!

Did you know that there are a lot of people setting up websites on "how-to" subjects and making a bundle from them? In addition to websites on this type of topic, go take a look on Amazon's Kindle store, there are literally thousands of "how to" eBooks, and even traditional print books too. My own books are a perfect example, and there are so many more than just me!

Tim Carter is a Nationally Syndicated Newspaper Columnist in the USA. He writes about "handyman" type subjects. How to build a deck. How to put gutters on your house, stuff like that. Now, being nationally syndicated, I am quite sure that Tim makes a good salary writing in newspapers. However, some time back, Tim put up a website of his own too. It is called "AskTheBuilder.com." On his website, Tim handles the same subject that he handles in his newspaper column. However, I have been told that Tim makes a lot more money from his website than he ever made from writing the newspaper column!

For his website, Tim makes Videos, and puts them up, along with a written explanation of the topic. For example, as I write this, the project that Tim is featuring is "how to cut ceramic tile." Tim has a written article about how to cut ceramic tile, but even better, he has a 3 minute video showing the entire process. For me, if I need to learn how to cut a ceramic tile, or some other kind of handyman subject, I will get a lot more out of a video than a written article. We all have different methods that work best for us to learn, and for me video, or one-on-one personal teaching is best. How about you?

One of the cool things about Tim's setup is that he is using YouTube to serve the videos, meaning that he doesn't even have to pay for the video bandwidth, since it is provided by a 3rd Party who will actually do it for free. In addition, YouTube is a recognized site that lends Tim credibility in the eyes of a lot of his potential viewers and readers.

Tim literally has hundreds (maybe thousands) of such projects available on his site, and they are all free. So, how does Tim make money? Well, he has Google AdSense on his site, and also other ads that he sells directly. And, believe me, Tim does very well with his direct ad sales! He is offering ads to individual sponsors ranging from $90 per month up to over $3,000 per month. If he sells only a few ads in that upper range, he has a real winner there! And, he does have such ads already sold, so he is not just dreaming!

Imagine how many different subjects could be set up on the web like this! Just about any subject on which you have expertise could be your personal site where you can literally rake in the profits.

There is also more than one way to monetize a setup like this. You could offer some free content, advertising supported, in addition to archives that you charge a small fee for. The number of ways that you can make money off such a site are almost limitless. Also, no matter how narrow the subject matter of the site, you will have an audience, provided that you really are an expert, and are willing to share what you know with others who want to learn. Remember also that even if you don't think you are an expert on a topic, as you get in and write about the topic you will continue to gain more expertise. For instance, when I first started my website about living in the Philippines, I just wrote about my opinion on things. Now, over the years, I am widely recognized as being one of the leading experts about the expat life in the country. This happened, because I am deeply involved in the topic, and I learn more every day that I work with the issues.

As another way to make money from the site, Tim even has his own store on the site where you can buy tools, supplies for builders and such. Having built up a trusting audience of readers, I am sure that Tim does very well with his store as well. Tim also sells e-Books with even more courses on how to get jobs done!

There are many others who have "Ask the Expert" sites, and the formula works! Another person who has been very successful with this type of site is a tech guru named Dave Taylor. As I say, there are others too, which just goes to show that this is a real potential money maker, if you can provide expertise on a subject that is in demand.

Something like this can turn into an excellent money maker for you, and I really encourage you to look at where your area of expertise is, and how you can capitalize on it!

# 14 – BUILD WEBSITES FOR YOUR PRODUCTS

In a previous edition of this book I had a chapter about MFA. What is MFA? Made For AdSense. AdSense, of course, is the Google advertising program. AdSense are "PPC" or Pay-Per-Click ads that you can put on your website. There was a time when AdSense could produce some very nice income.

Back in the 2004 to 2007 era or so, I used to regularly earn around $1,000 using Google AdSense each and every month. Now, that income has gone way, way down, and to be honest, I no longer consider AdSense to be worth my time. I still do keep AdSense on my smaller websites, especially websites for which I don't have any products of my own to sell. But, the amount of income that those sites bring in is so small that it is not even worth talking about.

When I say MFA, I am talking about a website that was Made For AdSense. In other words, you made the website for no other reason than to display ads from Google AdSense.

Now, though, I no longer consider that a worthwhile venture. What I would advocate now in this realm is to produce websites to support and sell products that you produce yourself.

For the most part, the products that I am talking about are things like eBooks, and some other digital products. Products that you can produce and sell, and can be delivered via email or direct download by the purchaser. The eBook is the prime example of such a product.

There are a couple of ways to look at such products, and how to come up with good ideas for such a product. The way that most people do it, which may or may not be the best way, is that they have a website, so they think of products that they can produce and sell to the readers of that site. For example, my biggest and most popular website, as I have mentioned many times in this book, is about living in the Philippines. As that site has developed that website over the years, I will think about what products would sell on the site.

I can look at the site, the readers of the site, and think to myself "what do these people need or want?" "What can I produce that would assist my readers?" These kinds of questions lead to ideas for new products to put on your existing website.

However, there is also a completely different way to go about this. You could think of products that are completely unrelated to your websites, produce the product and then make a website to support the product and sell it. Let's say that you get into a new hobby. You have suddenly developed a great interest in Frisbee. You have decided to write a couple of book about Frisbee, and you have plans on how a person can produce a new style of "super Frisbee". You have then written your books, and a PDF file with instructions on how to make this new Frisbee design. You have these new potential products ready to go, but nobody is buying them, because you have no sales channel on which to promote them.

Time to build a website! Since you have a great interest in Frisbees, you could probably develop a site where you would blog about Frisbees because with your great interest that has come about, this is a topic for which you have a passion. Once you start gaining a readership, you have a natural sales channel on that exact site.

Here is a bit of a side issue, though, to consider. Make sure that you have the right sales channel!

Over the years, as I became well known for providing information to people who want to move to the Philippines like I did, I started developing eBooks and other types of digital products. I used to be really into online auctions in a "previous life". As I have explained in this book, I used to be a pretty big seller on eBay. At that time, I purchased a domain name "Auctiontopia.com". I always liked the name a lot. Kind of a word that I coined on my own, a combination of "Auction" and "Utopia". It was a great domain name for writing about online auctions.

By the time that I got into the whole "move to the Philippines" niche and started writing books on the topic, I was really no longer using the Auctiontopia domain name, because I had moved on from online auction selling. But, I just really loved that domain name. I decided to use that domain for selling my books! I thought it was a great idea to do so. I thought the name was "catchy" and people would remember the name easily.

Well, maybe people who were auction sellers would remember the name, but I learned that my "move to the Philippines" readers really didn't care for the name and they really did not remember it.

My readers in the new niche didn't care about online auctions, what they cared about was that they wanted to become "expats" - people who would move to other countries and start a new life. I put up resistance, because I loved that Auctiontopia name. Finally, after urging that I got from a few friends, I quit being bull-headed and I made a change. I set up a really nice bookstore website on a new domain name - ExpatIsland.com. It almost instantly was a big hit. I sold many more books on the new domain compared to the old one. In fact, within 6 months after moving to the new domain name, my book sales had increased by 10 fold! I had not changed anything else, except to build a nicer bookstore site, and build it on a new domain name that was more closely aligned with the interests of my readers!

So, what I am encouraging you to do is to develop products, and build websites to promote and sell your products. I really prefer digital products if you can do that, but there is also money to be made on physical products too. Digital is just easier and cheaper. No hassles with shipping and such.

These days, the big gold rush in making money on the Internet is, in my view, through producing your own products! So, get started. It will take time to develop the audience and to develop the products, but the effort will certainly pay off!

# 15 – START A WEBSITE ABOUT THE PLACE WHERE YOU LIVE

Let's say that you settle down in Davao City, Philippines, or in Victoria, Canada. Start a website about the place. Offer every bit of information that you can about the place. This can really develop into a major resource for the area, and there are a number of ways for you to make money with such a setup.

Unless you live in a particularly urban area like New York City, Los Angeles, or Manila, you can likely build up your website into an authority on the area where you live. In those large cities, many such websites are likely to already exist.

Work on it diligently and keep building it up. Make yourself an authority on the area. Soon you will find that people will start coming to you looking for information on the area. When somebody is planning to come for vacation, they will email and ask what hotels they should consider. Maybe they will ask about getting a rental car. Maybe somebody from abroad is planning to marry a girl from your town, he might ask about wedding packages for the ceremony, reception, even the honeymoon. All of these are things that you can make money on.

How do you make the money? Well, there are a number of ways. First, get commissions. If you get regular inquiries for hotel stays, go around to local hotels and work out deals with them. Many such places will pay a 10% commission to you if you send referrals to them. Let's say that somebody comes and stays at a local hotel for 3 weeks, 21 days. Let's say that the room is $99 per night, which is not a high priced room. So, you could get $9.90 per night (10% commission), or a total of $207.90 for that one guest's stay. If you have 3 or 4 guests coming into town regularly, that can add up. And, you can get other commissions too. If the guy is coming for a wedding, help line up a Wedding planner to make all the arrangements, and don't forget a commission from him too!

Alternatively, you can make an even bigger amount if you get into these services yourself! Maybe your house could be turned into a bed and breakfast, or you could lease or purchase a building that would be such a business. Doing that, and keeping it full of guests that you lure in through your website could turn a really nice profit. Maybe you already own a bed and breakfast, but you are not getting as many bookings as you need to make a profit. By starting up such an "authority" website about your area, you might have just found the magnet that you need to lure in the visitors for your business.

Don't forget to ask for commissions or outright payments from any businesses that you feature on your website! Maybe you are located in the Colorado Rockies and you have a write-up about horseback riding on the mountain trails. You can expect for companies offering such recreation to pay you for referrals! The system of paying and earning commissions is as old as business itself! No reason to feel shy about requesting commissions about referrals that you are sending to other business people!

I know one Canadian fellow who moved to live in a rather rural part of the Philippines. The town where he was moving to basically had no hotels, so he built a house, which included guest rooms that he could treat as a hotel, or maybe you'd call it a "Bed & Breakfast." Whatever you call it, he regularly has guests staying there, and they pay for their rooms, and other services that he offers. The way I see it, I don't think that the guy is causing much grief or worry for the Hilton Hotels or any of the other big chains, but he is keeping his bills paid, and that is what is important to him!

Another thing you can do with your website is to offer advertising on it. For example, if there is a company in your area who is looking for tourist business, let them pay to advertise on your site! Let's say that somebody has set up a swimming pool or Gym where people can work out, that is a perfect type of business who would benefit from advertising on your site to attract business from tourists and visitors in the area. I have found that some of these types of businesses are scared to commit to putting out cash to advertise. In those cases, I have offered to do it on a commission basis, as I said in the case of hotels, and the people then know that they only pay if you actually produce business for them. In many cases, under this arrangement, I have found that I made more money than if the company had simply purchased an advertisement! You can use this strategy too.

By becoming an authority on the area where you live, it opens up a whole lot of opportunities to earn money based on people needing assistance in coming to visit the area. You will be surprised at the opportunities that will arise when you gain the kind of reputation that will come with authority!

# 16 – SELL INDIGENOUS PRODUCTS

No matter where you live in the world, somewhere within a relatively short distance you will find some kind of products and items that are indigenous to your area. If you live in Maine there is lobster. If you live in the State of Washington, where I used to live, they have jewelry products made out of the ash from Mt. St. Helens, the volcano. Every area has some type of unique product that is generally not available in other areas.

Find such products and sell them online. Some things may not be as good as others. My example of the lobster in Maine may be a very poor example. Firstly, because there are many people selling lobster from Maine. Secondly, because shipping live lobster might be quite tedious to do. However, something like my other example, the Volcanic Ash jewelry is easy to source, has little competition and is very easy to ship to any location in the world.

The fact is, if you live in a place where these certain items are not available, they are certainly looked upon as desirable, rare, and worth money. A piece of Mt. St. Helens ash jewelry may be very commonplace in Kelso, Washington or even in Portland, Oregon, but if you are in Memphis, Tennessee you may have never seen such an item. If Susie in Memphis saw a website selling necklaces with a Mt. St. Helens stone, she just might be very attracted to it.

The thing is, products like these are generally not available outside the area where they came from. You can sell them online, and have a very unique product that cannot be found elsewhere. Take advantage of this.

Now, you may be asking who would buy such things? Well, lots of people will. There are people who are collectors of such items worldwide, and they will buy the stuff. Perhaps somebody who has gone on vacation in the past in your area, and just wants to go back and purchase a remembrance of the trip. There are lots of people who will buy these kinds of items, to be honest.

Getting the items, if you live in the area is quite easy, and generally the prices, if you buy direct from the people making the items, are very low. It's a win-win situation, you can get quality, unique items at a cheap price. It's a perfect recipe for ecommerce success. All you have to do is get started!

I really feel that there is enough demand to justify your getting into this business, and the nice thing is that if others do it, that generally won't hurt you! Why? Because just 50 miles or 100 miles away, it is a different type of product from that area, and generally their products are totally different. So, a different store can be set up for each region without affecting sales from the others. As a matter of fact, one thing you could do is to work on becoming the "Superstore" for such products, or set up a mall, with each regional craft being sold, all in one place. The logistics of getting products from all over the country may be a little difficult to work out, but it can be done, if you work at it.

This is an opportunity that most people don't think of, because an item from near their home seems very commonplace and easy to get. But, when you get 500 miles or a few thousand miles away from the area, it might be a very rare and desirable item! Give this a try, the cost to try is so close to zero that I don't see any way you can lose!

# 17 – WEB HOSTING

What is Web Hosting? Well, basically it means that you would have a server on the Internet, and you will lease space to other people who wish to put up websites. Frankly, this is an easy and cheap business, although there are a lot of people doing it. The market is still big enough for many more players, though, and it's a business you should consider.

This is a business that I am personally in myself, and I can tell you that there is money to be made on this. Frankly, it's not as difficult as you might expect either. You see, you simply need to open up a reseller account with some bigger Web Hosting company, and then you are ready to go – you can re-sell the space that you have just leased. Now, there are accounts that you can set up for very low prices, even for $5 to $20 per month there are dozens of re-seller accounts. For me, though, I highly recommend going all out and setting up with a quality web host and get into some serious business, not just playing around.

I have two recommendations as to where you should set up your business:

**ServInt** – (www.servint.net) ServInt can provide you with a VPS (Virtual Private Server) for anywhere from $50 to $250 or more. I have been hosting my sites on a ServInt server for many years now, and I've only rarely had outages or other problems with their service. This is saying a lot, because many web hosting companies don't offer good service, so when you find a good one that is giving good service, it's important to stick with them! Yes, ServInt is not cheap, but you should also consider the old adage - "you get what you pay for." Basically, for a server that is $50 or so, you could expect to set up 100 or more clients on it, depending on how they are using their space, and how popular their sites are. For me, I provide premium hosting, and I also charge a premium price for the service. I give people quality service, but I charge them a price that is higher than the "cheap guys." For example, my low end account is P1000 per month (about $25), whereas they could get a similar service for maybe 1/5 that price. Mine is more reliable, and I offer much better customer service, though, which is why I am able to charge a premium price.

If you are hosting with ServInt, one thing to keep in mind – it is up to you to provide technical and customer service support for your clients. ServInt will provide this kind of support to YOU, but not to your clients. If you are not comfortable in handling this type of service to clients, I have a second solution for you.

**Digital Ocean** – (www.digitalocean.com). DigitalOcean is a "cloud hosting" provider. What is cloud hosting? Read this:

Cloud hosting is based on the most innovative Cloud computing technologies that allow unlimited number of machines to act as one system. Other hosting solutions (shared or dedicated) depend on one machine only, while cloud hosting security is guaranteed by many servers.

Instead of having your own server, your account is spread on to multiple servers to help balance the load of your accounts amongst the entire network instead of just one machine. I have used DigitalOcean only a short time as I write this (a few months now), but so far I have been quite satisfied with the service they are providing me.

An account with DigitalOcean ranges from $5 per month to over $600 per month. You need to review their plans and match what you pay with your needs for hosting. For a starter, you should be nearer to the lower end of the pricing scale.

One thing I do is that I host my own websites on DigitalOcean or ServInt, and I host client accounts. Thus, it basically give me a free server for my sites, all the while making money for me! I believe that the hosting business will fit nicely for almost anybody who wants to give it a try. You can not only host your own sites this way for no additional cost, you can actually make money by hosting your clients as well! How can you lose? I especially like the fact that with multiple hosting clients you can afford to invest in high quality servers, which will give you great fast and reliable hosting for your own sites as well.

# 18 – BUY AN EXISTING WEBSITE THAT IS EARNING MONEY

Buy a website that is already earning money!

Yes, believe it or not, you can actually purchase an existing website that is already earning money, and start operating it yourself, thus earning the money yourself.

Why would somebody sell a site that is earning money already? Maybe they are tired of it. Maybe they feel it isn't earning enough to keep their interest. There can be any number of reasons.

The neat thing about this is that after you have done this for a while you will learn what is bringing in money on the site. The more you do it, the more you will learn, and you will find that soon you can purchase a website (or start a new site of your own) and quickly and easily double or triple the earnings with just a few simple changes. For instance a site might be earning $1,000 per month. If you do some things to garner some extra visits, increase click-throughs and such, after just a few months you can easily increase the earnings of the site.

Be careful about what type of site you buy, though. For instance, some of my sites are really keyed in on ME. People read the site because they like me, and like to read what I write. I have other sites where the visitors really don't care much about ME, what they care about is the subject matter. They will read it whether I write it, or if Joe Blow writes it. You want to buy a site where people don't care so much who the author is. If you bought one of my sites where the people cared what I said, and suddenly I was gone and you started doing the writing, you could quickly end up with a site but no visitors! If that happened, all the earnings would also likely dry up.

Purchasing a site and improving it is a good strategy. However, just be careful what you are buying. Make sure that the site traffic and earnings really are what is claimed, and make sure that you are getting a site that will transfer over to you without pushing away all the visitors.

Another thing to be aware of when you buy a site, is to make sure of what you are buying. Some sellers might think you get the domain name and nothing else. Others might feel that you get the domain name and also all the content on the site. For me, I feel that if you buy an existing website you want the content and everything associated with the website! Taking less than that could turn out to be a bad move.

So, how do you find websites that are for sale? There are several good sources.

The big one that has been around for a long time is called Flippa. There are many websites listed for sale there, so you should check them out.

Another site where you can find websites for sale is operated by a couple of friends of mine. Their names are Justin and Joe. Justin and Joe (I mostly know Justin as a friend, only an acquaintance of Joe's) are Americans, like me, but they moved to Davao some years back and lived here for probably 5 to 7 years or so. Both of them are now living a "location independent" lifestyle, traveling a lot and such. Their website that markets websites is called "Empire Flippers" - drop by and see what they have for sale. I trust Justin and Joe, and I don't believe that they will steer you wrong.

Buying an existing site might be just the right thing for a newbie, something to get started with. You can learn a lot on how to get your own website off the ground by operating an ongoing site, and this might be your chance to do just that!

# 19 – BUILDING A COMMUNITY ON THE INTERNET

A community? On the Internet? What is this all about? Isn't a community like a place to live, a town, a city?

Well, indeed it is. However, a community can be other things as well. Any place (real place or virtual place) where people gather and interact with each other can be a community. There are many communities online on the Internet, and this book is here to talk about building communities.

We will be looking at a few questions, and hopefully a lot of answers as well. What are some examples of online communities? Should you join online communities? More importantly, should you try to build an online community of your own? Can having an online community help you make money? If so, how?

These are all questions that we will delve into in this book. So, let's get started by asking a few questions and also answering them.

What are some examples of Online Communities?

Well, the truth is that much of the Internet that we all know and use revolves around online communities. Not everything on the Internet is a community, but much of it is. Let's look at it by examining just one site that is very popular, YouTube.

When YouTube first got started, it really was not so much of a community. It was a place where people could upload videos that they produced, and other people could watch those videos.

Today, though, YouTube is much more of a community than just a place to post and watch Videos. For example, I have my own "Channel" on YouTube, it is called the "MindanaoBob Channel".

MindanaoBob is a nickname that many people call me by. How did I get that nickname? Well, my name is Bob, and I live on the Island of Mindanao, and some years ago, some people started calling me "MindanaoBob" and the nickname stuck, so I started using it for things like my YouTube Channel. It sort of became my trademark. But, that is all kind of irrelevant to this book, so let's forge forward.

So, I have my MindanaoBob Channel on YouTube, and all of my videos there are about my life in the Philippines. As people see my videos, and they like them, then they subscribe to my Channel. When they subscribe to my YouTube Channel, they get things like e-mail updates informing them whenever I upload a new video. Since these people are kind of my "fans" and enjoy my videos, when they get notified of my new video, most of them go and check out what I just uploaded.

Also, on YouTube, in addition to subscribing to my Channel, people can also make me one of their "friends" and we can communicate with each other. When somebody wants to be friends with me on YouTube, they indicate that they want that, and YouTube sends me an e-mail telling me that somebody wants to be my friend. At that point, I can choose whether I want to be friends with them, which in almost every case I choose to be friends.

Many times, if the person who subscribes to my video also has their own YouTube Channel, I will check out their videos, and if their video topic is of interest to me, I will return the favor and subscribe to their channel as well. When I subscribe to their channel, the people who have subscribed to my channel can see that I am now subscribed to a new channel, and they will go check it out and make a connection with that new person as well, growing two communities at once! As this sort of thing grows and grows, and my viewers get interconnected with the people that I subscribe to, a community begins to form. This is what community on the Internet is all about. People with similar interests are drawn together into their own little "virtual community," they get to know each other, inter-subscribe with each other, trade ideas, and soon it is a thriving community!

The Internet is filled with tens of thousands, maybe millions of sites that foster the creation of such communities online, bringing people together. Once people join into such a community, they tend to stay there too, as long as they maintain an interest for the subject matter that brought the community together. Of course, each topic has many communities. For example, as I said, my YouTube Channel is centered around videos of life in the Philippines, since that is where I live, and what I make videos about. Now, there are lots of other communities about living in the Philippines, my community is only one such community. There are thousands of other video publishers on YouTube who also put out videos about the Philippines, and each of those publishers has his own little community on YouTube. Also, there are other websites outside of YouTube on the topic as well, and these each have their own community on the topic. Sometimes, two different communities on the same topic (or even more than two) will interact with each other. Although the communities are separate, they interact, and have some common members too.

In fact, my YouTube Channel is only a sub-community. What do I mean? Well, I mean that my real Community of those who are interested in the topic of living in the Philippines includes my YouTube Channel, it also includes a Fan Page on Facebook, a bunch of people who follow me on Twitter, and my own Website, which is the Live in the Philippines Web Magazine. Many of the people in my community follow all facets of my community that I listed. Other people follow only one or two of my sub communities. But, overall, I would consider each of those "arms" to be part of my greater community. I guess you could say that each of them is a "neighborhood" in my community.

Another important thing to consider is that by having each of these sub-communities, or neighborhoods, it helps make people aware of my greater community. For example, if somebody finds one of my videos on YouTube and he likes it, he will visit my Channel, and subscribe to it. As he looks over my YouTube Channel, he will find links and references to my Facebook page, my Twitter account and my Web Magazine. If he really enjoys the topic that I am writing about, or shooting videos about, he has the opportunity to join each of these neighborhoods to take advantage of the entire greater community. This helps me achieve more success by bringing in more people into each neighborhood of my community!

Another thing to consider is that the more neighborhoods you set up in your community, and the more information you publish on each sub-community, it helps set you up as an expert in the field. When people see that you have so many facets in your community, they will put more stock in what you say, and consider you as more of a "go to" person for information than others who don't build their community as well as you do.

For example, if you set up a Website, a YouTube Channel, a Facebook Fan Page, a Twitter account and all of the other available "neighborhoods", but a competitor has only a blog, well, a lot more people are going to find you and end up following you as an authority in that field of knowledge. There can be no doubt about that.

Remember, though, just setting up all of these things does not make your community vibrant. For example, if you set up a YouTube Channel, a Facebook page and a Blog, but you never make any new videos, never update your Facebook status, and only post on your blog irregularly, well, your community will not be very compelling. Also, even if you do these things regularly, if you don't interact with your subscribers and readers, they will not keep coming back for very long.

Should you try to establish your own Online Community?

So, a lot of big sites like YouTube, Facebook and such have online communities. But, the question you may be asking is whether you should try to create your own online community. Maybe you are asking how you could even go about creating an online community since you are only a small player, and don't have the "big bucks" like these big websites have.

*Having an online community can be bad.*

Yes, it's true, and I'll be the first to tell you that there are actually bad aspects to having an online community! It's true! If you create a very close and active online community on your website, it can actually cause you to make less money

What? You can make less money by having a very active and loyal following?

Without a doubt, the answer is yes.

Let's say that you have a website that has 3,000 hard core fans who come and visit your site each and every day. Let's say that I have a website that really doesn't have any real fans at all, but still gets 400 visitors each and every day, albeit very few visitors who come back again. Fact is, that I may make more money than you do, even though I have only a fraction of the readership that you have!

How can it be?

Well, have you ever heard of the term "ad blindness?" Ad blindness is something that happens when a person visits the same website over and over again, every day, or several times per week. You have advertising on your website (that's one of the ways that you make money after all!), but these rabid fans who come to your website every day (sometimes more than once per day) will likely stop seeing them! They will, frankly, become blind to the ads. Why? Because they have seen the ads so many times that their mind will block them out, and the ads will not even be seen or noticed anymore.

There are things that you can do to overcome ad blindness, though, and I will be going over some of those things later in this chapter.

So, ad blindness is one of the reasons why a very community oriented website may actually cause you to lose money. So, does that mean that you should do what you can to avoid having your site become an online community?

Personally, I think that is not a good idea.

Why should you still strive to build an Online Community.

So, even though I have pointed out why it might cost you money to have an online community, I still think that you should strive very hard to establish your site as a community oriented site.

Why would I say that?

Because, the truth is, that if you do things right, in the long run you can recover the lost earnings, and increase the earnings exponentially. You will, over the longer term, make a lot more money with an online community.

The fact is that when you create a loyal community of readers who think of you as an expert in the field of your writing, and also consider you as a fellow member of the community and a friend, your credibility with your readers can lead to earnings a lot bigger than your might lose under the previous example that I explained.

The money that you will lose, initially, will be from things like Pay Per Click Advertising, things like Google AdSense. As I explained, your readers will become blind to those ads. However, by becoming an expert in the field, and having fiercely loyal readership, you are opening the doors to other revenue sources.

I believe that your number one goal once you establish community should be to write a series of e-Books (like this one) that you can sell to your readers. They think of you as an expert, and a book on a topic that they love, from an expert is very valuable, and a very good source of income for you. They also think of you as a fellow community member, and a friend, and thus they will want to buy your book, because they can not only learn from you, but they can support a friend, and help him out too. So, write a number of books on the topic of your community's interest, and sell them to your followers. This is something that will make you a lot more money than the Pay Per Click advertising anyway.

In another chapter of this book I actually tell you how you can write an e-book yourself and self publish it too. You can sell only one tenth the number of copies that a publisher could sell for you, and make nearly 20 times as much money! That's right, sell a lot fewer books, and make more money, and with the power of the online community this is all possible, even probable. You can do it, but only if you try! In fact, in that chapter, I tell you how you can make $50,000 per year with just a few e-Books.

In fact, writing e-Books and selling them to your community is only one way to make money from your online community. There are plenty of others too.

Services – You can sell services to your community. For example, in my online community which is about living in the Philippines, my wife and I sell a lot of services. My wife sells Real Estate in the Philippines and earns commission doing so. There have been months where she has worked only a few hours in the month and made as much as $4,000 selling only to members of my online community. In fact, most of the time, she averages monthly commissions in the range of $2,000 each month while working less than a few days per month. All of this is possible only because of our online community, and if we did not have an online community, her earnings on the Real Estate would be zero.

Consulting – Again, if people need assistance in your area of expertise, and they are aware of, or are a member of your online community, you can consult with them, helping them solve their problem or just giving them advice. I personally do telephone consulting to my online community members, and I charge $100 per hour for my consulting work. To date, all of my consulting work has been working with people who are members of my online community. My wife, in addition to her Real Estate sales, also operates a business where she does "Relocation Consulting" for members of our online community. When somebody in our community makes the decision to move to and live in the Philippines, my wife will assist them in making the move, finding a house to buy or rent, show them around town, help them with any needs in making such a big International move. She makes nice money doing this too.

The fact is, there are many other types of side-businesses you can do to serve your online community members, it just depends on the topic of interest to your community. I personally have dozens of different businesses serving my online community.

All of these businesses would not be possible if I just had a "regular website" where people came to visit once or twice only. But, because I have built community, established a relationship of trust with my fellow community members, and demonstrated my expertise in their area of interest, people have flocked to the businesses that I have offered. You can do it too, if you are willing to take the time to build that community.

So, as you can see, you might lose some money when it comes to the Pay Per Click type of advertising, but the benefits of building an Online Community are huge and will pay you a lot more than you will ever lose. And.. to be honest, over the long haul, you can get back the Pay Per Click earnings too, and I'll show you how to do it.

## Conquering Ad Blindness

As I explained previously, if you have regular visitors who come to your website every day, or possibly multiple visits per day, it is likely that those loyal fans are already blind to ads. They are blind to Pay Per Click ads like AdSense, and they are even blind to ads for your own products like e-Books, Consulting or other services that you may offer.

But, Bob, in the previous section you said that I should write e-Books, do consulting, offer services in order to make more money, since I won't make as much from AdSense. Now you are saying that the loyal readers will be blind to ads for my services too? What gives? How can I make real money then?

Well, yes, you are right, I did say that you should do some of those things (or all of them), and I also said that your loyal "fan" type of readers will be blind to those ads as well as AdSense. But, you can combat it!

How do you combat ad blindness? You change things up! You periodically change the colors on your ads. You change the positions of the ads. You sometimes run with no ads at all. You set up rules of when certain types of ads will show up. I like to use a WordPress plug-in called "Ad Injection" which is available for free for your WordPress Self-Hosted Blog.

With "Ad Injection" you can set up all kinds of rules to determine when ads are shown, when they are not shown, who sees them, who doesn't see them, what type of ads are shown given certain conditions and such. It is an amazing tool that will allow you to really "trick" the reader into seeing the types of ads that they will respond to. For example, you could say that if the reader is a regular reader of the site, only show him the ad for your new eBook. If the reader is not a regular (and thus does not already realize that you are a guru on the topic!), then show him AdSense. Did you know that your non-regular readers, especially those who find you by using a search engine are the most likely to click on an AdSense ad? So, use the plug-in to show the ads to those kinds of people!

But, Bob, you already said the regular readers do not see the ads, even for your e-Books and such. Why are you going to show him the e-Book ads?

How much will you earn from selling your own e-Book? Well, the answer is relatively simple. He may be unlikely to see the ad, but if he does, at least he sees an ad that you are going to make some really nice money with! I mean, if he happens to see an AdSense ad and clicks on it, you are likely to make only 10 cents to a Dollar or so (sometimes you will make more than that for a click, but not usually). If he sees your e-Book ad and pays you $30 for an e-Book, you made a lot nicer payday.

But, wait, did you know that I have another method to make sure that those loyal "fan" type readers will also know about my eBooks? Yes, indeed I do. What I do is mix in information about my e-Books (and other products) right into my articles on my site!

As an example, a while back, I got an e-mail from a fellow who was looking for how to get a job in the Philippines, so that he could move and live here like I do. He badly wanted to live in the Philippines, but he didn't have any money in savings to make such a move possible. So, he wrote and asked me how to get a job here. I responded to him by writing an article on my website on the subject. I explained that it is nearly impossible for a foreigner to get a job in the Philippines, and that even if you are a very lucky person and find an actual job, that the salaries here are very low, usually just a few dollars per day.

But, do you know what else I did? You see, I have this e-Book that I wrote about 3 years ago called "49 Ways to Make a Living in the Philippines" which explains ways to start your own businesses (mostly online businesses) in the Philippines and make enough money to have a nice life here. The book is $49, just $1 for each idea that I spell out. Well, at the end of this article about finding jobs in the Philippines, I put a section telling about my book, and I offered a coupon so that anybody who read the article and wanted the book could get it for just $29, a big savings of $20, but for a limited time only. So, you see, it wasn't really an ad that was outside the place where people normally concentrate their reading efforts. It was a mention of the book, right inside the article, that a lot of people read. And, do you know what? I sold a lot of books in just a few days' time when I did that. A lot of the people who bought it were long time loyal fans of the site too, even though the book had already been on the market for 3 years! So, you see, there are ways to eliminate ad blindness!

For ads like AdSense, as I said earlier, you can still do things to make your loyal readers see the ads from more. Change the colors of the ads. Move the ads to a different position on the site every now and then. All of these types of things "shake up" the readers and end up making you a bit of extra money on AdSense for a while, while people are growing accustomed to the site again. After all, when you make these changes, people must "re-train" their eyes to the "new look".

Speaking of the "new look" I have also had great success in eliminating ad blindness by re-designing my site from time to time. Do a complete makeover of the site – new colors and an entire new look. For me, though, I only do it once per year or even a bit less than that. I like to keep a feeling of continuity on the site, and keep things the same, but once per year, or every year and a half or so, I shake things up with a complete redesign. When I do this, I get a nice spike in my AdSense earnings for sometimes several months after such a change.

So, as you see, ad blindness can be combated. You can also effectively sell your own products and services to your loyal readers, your online community very effectively, and in the course of doing that, you can really spark your profits to spectacular levels.

## How do you build the online community?

How do you do it? Well, it takes time. Personally, I feel that the fastest that you could really build a decent community of readers and fans online is probably about one year or so. I feel that in most cases it will take longer than that, maybe two years. And, you must be very active and keep doing the right things, even when you have no readers to speak of. But, if you can do it, and stick to it, you will end up prospering in the long run, without a doubt.

So, how? First thing, you need to choose a topic to write about that is something that you are very passionate about. You also need to be very knowledgeable about the topic too. Choose a topic that you really can keep writing about even when it seems that nobody is reading your articles. If you can keep it up, the community will come. It just takes time.

In my case, for my most effective online community (I actually have several in completely different niche subjects) is, as I have mentioned, about living in the Philippines. Let's look at how I used that niche to build up a large online community. You can look at what I did with my niche, choose your own topic and copy, or adapt what I did in ways that will work for you.

I started out in 2006 by establishing a website called "Live in the Philippines." I put up a blog on the site and wrote about my daily life and what it was like to live in the Philippines. The topic of living in the Philippines is a very narrow niche topic, because frankly, there are not a lot of people who want to live in the Philippines, in the grand scheme of things. Certainly only a fraction of one percent of people have ever even considered living in the Philippines.

When I first started the site, I got few, if any readers who came to read my articles. At the beginning, I wrote very infrequently. Sometimes I wrote only one article per month. Sometimes I went more than a month without writing a single article! But, as time went by, after about 6 months of writing, and after having maybe 20 or 25 articles on the site, I started noticing that I was getting a few comments from actual readers. This encouraged me, and I began writing on a regular schedule, at least one article per day. I kept this up for about 2 months and witnessed my readership increase dramatically.

When I added my wife as a writer on my blog, traffic increased!

After about 3 months of posting daily articles on my blog, and often twice per day articles, I got an idea to increase the number of articles on my blog, and also increase the amount of interest by having my wife also write on the site. I figured that my wife was going through the same daily process that I was, of living in the Philippines, which is what my site was about. However, two different people could experience the exact same things in their lives and have different feelings and different reactions to the experience. So, I decided that adding my wife as a writer on the site would offer a sort of point/counterpoint type of point of view to the site. It worked!

After a couple of months of having my wife as a second writer on the site, I saw that things were going well, and my readership, albeit a small group at the time, seemed to be really happy to have her on the site! I thought more about this and thought about other ways that I could improve the site. After realizing that adding my wife was a good move, I thought to myself that adding other writers might be a good thing as well. So, I decided that adding other foreigners who had moved to live in the Philippines might add additional value to the site.

So, I started recruiting others to write on my site. I wanted to have a diverse group of writers. People from different backgrounds. People from different countries, etc. The diversity would lead to a diversity of opinion and feeling of what it was like to live in the Philippines, and would thus add more value for my readers. It did not take long and I picked up several new writers. I got a fellow from the UK and a German to join the writing team. Next, I got an Australian, and other Americans like me. My writing team kept growing, and the number of and diversity of articles on the site expanded exponentially. It turned out that it was really a good thing for the site, and my readers loved it. Not only did my existing readers love it, but my number of readers started blossoming and pretty soon the site began sprouting into the online community that I keep telling you about.

There are other things you need to do, though, to get your site off of the ground. In the beginning of your site, there won't be many, or even any people following you. I have two critical recommendations to get you started down the road to popularity.

Firstly, you need to seek out other websites on the same niche topic, and start joining the conversation there. Leave comments about the articles. But, leave insightful comments, not just "spammy" types of comments. Say things that matter and give information, and are directly related to the information that the author wrote. The way that blogs work, your comment will have a link back to your website. As people notice your comments, and find them insightful, they will follow your link and go visit your site. It is important that you make certain that your site is fresh, with accurate information, so that when these people come to visit there is good material there to captivate them. If you start sending people over to your site and all they see is "Under Construction" or something like that, you won't make a good impression or gain a new regular reader. Also, make sure that the site is updated regularly. For example, if you are going around and leaving comments on other sites, and people start following your links to your site, but every time they go there, even weeks later, they find the same old articles, well, they won't keep coming. So, post up new articles on a regular basis.

I say to post articles on a regular basis, and this is very important. But, I also want to mention something that I learned over time with my own site. I learned that it is important to post articles on a regular schedule. For example, on my site, I post two new articles per day, five days per week. So, ten new articles each week, without fail. And, I post the articles at a regularly scheduled time each day. I post Mondays through Fridays. One new article goes up at 5am and a second article goes up at 5pm. I found that by posting on a strict time schedule like this, my readers flock to the site at those times to see what is new. If I don't keep a schedule, traffic on the site is more sporadic, and usually some people forget to visit for that day. So, for me, posting on a schedule is very important, and I believe it should be important for you too.

However, even with all of these suggestions, I believe that there is one very important thing that you really must do if you want to create an online community of your own. What is it?

**Interact with your readers**

Interacting with your readers is one of the best things you can do!

Yes, interact! What does that mean? What I mean is that when somebody leaves a comment on your article, you need to respond to the person. You don't always have to agree, but even if you disagree you show your reader the respect of responding to what he or she says. This is very important, and frankly, I can't stress it enough. If you don't reply back to comments that you get, it sends the message that you don't really care too much about what the reader told you.

Think about it, in any community, whether online or in the real world, communication is what makes the community what it is. If nobody talked to each other or interacted with each other at all, well, it wouldn't be much of a community, it would be more of a bunch of people living their own existence without regard for the others in their presence. If you don't take the time and effort to respond to the people who are reading your articles and commenting on them, then you are not fostering a relationship with that reader, and in the end, he will go off to some other community where his thoughts are shown more appreciation.

When you respond to your readers' comment, you need to do it on a timely basis too. In my case, I try to respond to all comments within one hour after they are left, unless they make the comment overnight while I am sleeping, or if I am away from my office. For the most part, though, I believe that those in my community would say that I do a good job of interacting with them.

A while back, I decided that I was going to cut back on replying to comments on my site. My site had gotten very large, and the number of comments was mind blowing. On an average article I could get up to 200 or 250 comments. Responding to that many comments is a job, almost a full time job. I told my readers that I was going to start replying only to comments which I felt I needed to reply to with information that would add value to the site. One of my readers responded by telling me the following (I am paraphrasing him):

Bob, there is something about your site that makes me want to hear what you have to say about my comment. Not only do I feel a need to comment on your articles, but I also need to see what you have to say about my comment. After commenting, I check back frequently to see what you have to say back to me. If you stop commenting it will make me mad. In fact, when I comment on other sites, it doesn't matter much to me if there is a response to what I say, in fact I don't even usually go back to see what was said in response. But, with your site, if I don't have a response in a rather short amount of time, I actually feel mad about that sometimes!

Can you guess why this fellow felt this way? Why did he get mad if I did not respond to him, while he didn't care much on other sites? It's actually quite a simple question to answer if you think it over. He got mad because he felt a connection to me, and it was important for him to know that I read his comment, and also to find out what I thought about it. In short, he felt part of a community, not just a random reader of a blog. Community is very powerful, and can really help establish you as a personality on the Internet, even if it is only a personality within a relatively small niche.

Based on that comment, I re-evaluated my idea of cutting back on my comment replies. As I thought about it, responding to messages was almost like a job, it kept me so busy. But... wait... I was making a good deal of money from this website just like a job too. So, I decided that in order to keep my community growing and to make my readers feel more appreciated, it was only appropriate that I reply to their comments, as a member of the community.

I also do other things to build community among my readers. Some of those things are very simple things. Many of my community members are my friends on Facebook. When it is their birthday (Facebook tells me who is having a birthday, as long as they have entered the date into Facebook), I send them a greeting to wish them a Happy Birthday. This is simple, but it is important in making these people feel that I care about them and am thinking of them, as a member of our mutual community. So simple, yet also very effective in fostering the kind of community atmosphere that I am looking for. I believe that you should do these kinds of small things in order to develop your own community too. I am sure that if you try it, you will find it very effective.

If you want to have your own online community, you can do it, but it is hard work, and work that you must do. There are no shortcuts. You can't take the right steps for a month but then give up because the community did not yet materialize. No, you have to do the work for the long haul. It will take at least a year of steady work to develop the community, and more likely it will take at least two years, possibly longer. But, if you are serious about it and you want to do it, you can do it. I firmly believe that.

Good luck in your community building efforts, and keep working!

# 20 – SHOULD YOU MAKE YOUR SITE A MEMBERSHIP SITE?

What is a membership website? Well, it is a site where people have to pay money to become a member before they can access the information on the site. Let me correct that a bit. Usually, there will be limited access to the site for free, enough information for the reader to get a "taste" of what he will find on the site, but if he wants the real information he will need to pay money in order to be able to read that. Frankly, usually the amount of free information is only enough to leave the reader wanting or needing more, and feeling a need or desire to pay to get the information that he wants or needs.

Is a membership website feasible? Can it really be done? Well, yes, it is feasible, but it is not always the right thing to do.

Here is a rule of thumb. In my opinion, you never want to make your primary website a membership site. You want that primary website to be a showcase of you and your work. People who come to your primary site and learn who you are and become a fan are likely to buy things from you, but if they don't ever get that introduction to who you are, they will probably never spend any money with you. And, as far as this book is concerned, your primary goal with your websites is to make money. By charging money for your premier site, you will never give people a chance to see who you are and what kind of information you can provide, let alone the quality of the information that you will give.

So, basically, in this case, I am here to tell you that you are going to be able to make more money by giving something away for free! Yes, it's true, but developing your "showcase" site and making it free, you will show off to people who you are, what you are all about, the quality of what you can provide to people and such, and by giving all of that away for free, you will, in turn, make it possible to start up other niche sites that you can actually charge money for!

Having said all of this, though, I do not believe that membership sites are a bad thing. I really do believe that there are sites that should be membership sites, and there are ways to do things that will make having a membership site beneficial for you and your wallet.

**A case study – My Experience**

Let me get into this discussion by looking at my own experience in this realm over the past years. I have had a lot of websites over the years, and I actually still have a lot of sites, although I have cut back my number of websites in the past few years to some extent. There was a time, for a few years when I was operating more than 200 different websites at a single time! The vast majority of those sites were not very popular sites, but they served the purpose of why I set them up, which was to draw a small audience and make a bit of money from Google AdSense through these sites. I never intended them to be huge or popular sites, I wanted them to be low-work sites that produced, in combination, a bit of income. I built this up to where by combining these small sites, I earned around $1,000 per month from Google AdSense, and I also earned around $200 per month from other Advertising opportunities on these small sites. So, for sites that I had to do little or no work, I was able to bring in about $1,200 per month. In addition to these tightly focused niche sites, I also had a number of big e-commerce sites, and also a rather large and popular blog, Mindanao Magazine, which really did not make much money, given the size of its readership. However, even though it did not make me a lot of money, Mindanao Magazine was really my showcase site, and I became somewhat well known because of that site.

In 2006, though, I started up a new blog site called Live in the Philippines. I started small with Live in the Philippines. The subject of the site was all about what it was like for a foreigner (like me!) to live in the Philippines. When I started the site up, I posted articles on the site only rarely, even as little as only once per month or so. After a few months, I increased my writing on the site to one article per week or so, and I started seeing a few readers showing up on the site. It encouraged me to see the readership of this new site grow, and I again increased my writing frequency on the site to the point where I wrote two articles per day, every single day on the site! The site began to flourish a bit, and soon I asked my wife to join me by writing on the site, to add a different perspective than just mine. Her addition to the site was well received by the readers, and again I was quite happy.

About 8 or 9 months from the birth of this site, I started inviting other expats to write on the site, about their lives in the Philippines. Soon, I had a stable of about a dozen writers for the site offering diverse opinions on all subjects related to expat life in the Philippines. At this point, because the site had become much more than "just a blog," I decided to change the name of the site to the Live in the Philippines Web Magazine (also known as LiP), and a great new site was born!

Over the years, the popularity of this Web Magazine grew and grew, and frankly, it really eclipsed my Mindanao Magazine site in terms of creating an audience for me. I developed a huge number readers, and my online popularity grew exponentially. It got to the point where if I went out anywhere in public, a lot of people knew who I was, because they had read my LiP site. I was very pleased with the success of the site.

LiP had become great in terms of making me something of a "celebrity" within the niche I was writing in. But, in terms of income, it just was not paying off that well. Oh, I made $1,000 to $1,500 per month from LiP, but if you looked at the amount of time I was devoting to the site, the payoff was very small. I really should have been making a multiple of that amount from the site, given the fact that I was devoting so much time to it.

At one point, I received an e-mail from a regular reader of the site, and he told me that he loved LiP, but he encouraged me that if I wanted to make more money from the site, I really should turn it into a membership site. At first, I didn't think it sounded like a good idea, but as I thought about it over a number of days and weeks, I became convinced that indeed, I should turn LiP into a site where readers must pay money to become a member if they wanted to read the articles.

As I analyzed my site, looking at the number of readers per article, and the comments left, it was clear to me that the vast majority of readers were showing the greatest interest in the articles that I wrote myself. At the time, I was writing 5 articles per week, one new article each weekday. I had other writers who were writing one article each per week, one of which was published each weekday, and two each on weekends. But, articles that I wrote myself got nearly triple the readership of the next most popular writer after me.

So, as I devised a plan on how to turn the site into a membership site, I decided that I wanted to offer a combination of free content combined with Premium Content which was available only for a price. On the Premium Content, though, anybody could read the first couple of paragraphs without paying anything. If they wanted to read the entire article, though, they must pay to become a member of the site.

Because there was greater interest in the articles that I wrote, I decided that instead of writing 5 free articles per week, I would offer two free articles per week, and my other 3 articles would be paid Premium Content. All of the articles from the other writers would remain free. This way, there was still a lot of free content for everybody to read, but if they wanted the most "in demand" articles, those would require payment.

I went so far as to announce to my readers the plan for making parts of the site a Premium paid site. Honestly, there was a lot of support from the readers. About 70% of those who commented on the plan were supportive and understood the move. Some of those who were supportive said that they would not opt to pay, but it was still OK to make the change. But, it did appear that there was enough of a positive feeling that there was certainly money to be made. I decided to make the move within a week.

However, over the next couple of days, I kept thinking about a few of the comments that were somewhat negative about the change. I felt bad about some people feeling negative about it, and I kept analyzing what they said. In the end, I changed my mind and decided to make some other changes to the site, but not to make it a paid site at all.

Instead of charging a fee for the content on the site, I decided to keep it free. In the process, though, I decided to step back from the site a bit as well. I was still an active writer on the site, but instead of offering 5 new articles per week, I cut my writing back to only 3 new articles every week, letting other writers fill in on those other two days. So, there were still the same number of articles, only I was personally writing a bit less.

With the extra time that I gained by decreasing my writing on the site, I focused on using the site to create additional streams of income. In the past, I had pretty much relied mostly on Google AdSense to monetize the site. I used my extra time to begin doing other things. I wrote some e-books on the topic of the site. I assisted my wife with monetizing her work on the site (she started offering additional services – for a fee – to our readers) and other means of deriving additional income from an already very popular site. All of this took time, but it worked! I was able to build the site's monetization to the point where I was earning as much as $6,000 per month from the site, even while doing less work! So, in this case, by not charging for the site, I was able to make more money. However, does that mean that you should never charge for your content on the Internet? NO, it does not mean that at all.

You see, LiP had become my showcase. It was through LiP that I was able to build a large audience of followers and fans, and I needed to keep that showcase open and free if I wanted to keep building on my business success. I could develop other sites that would generate income, either by charging membership fees, or through other means. This is what I did, and I believe that it is what you should do as well. In no case should you ever start off with a Membership Site, you need something that will build a following, and those people will be willing to spend money once they realize that you have something special to offer. So, I believe that you should follow that path, and that is where you will find success.

**Where I am today - some 6 to 8 years later**

As I noted above, I began developing other sites, related to the niche, where I could charge money for. Among those other sites, I have 4 or 5 membership sites. However, my original vision was to have sites where I would write articles for people to read, but they would have to pay to read those articles.

Over the years, I changed my thinking on that. Now, those membership sites that people must pay to join are mostly online courses - learning sites. People pay to learn something through a course. Right now, my most successful membership site is called "Learn a Philippine Language", a site where we have online courses to teach various languages used in the Philippines. Primarily we teach the Cebuano language, since I learned that language between 2007 through 2011. People pay $14.99 per month to be part of the site, and there are complete lessons on the language. The lessons include videos, MP3 audio that they can listen to anywhere, and flash cards.

Additionally, I have sites that feature courses where people can learn about culture and other things. Some people develop membership sites that have thousands, even tens of thousands of members paying monthly. Most of my membership sites only get a few new members per month. Maybe I am earning $100 to $300 or so each month from these mini-membership sites, but when you add them all up, it does make a nice supplement to my income. And, once you make the courses, there is little, if anything, that you must do to keep the site running and bringing in income.

**The Mechanics – How to do it**

Anybody who knows much about me knows that I build all of my websites on the WordPress platform. WordPress is an open source software package that was originally designed for blogging. However, today WordPress is used widely not only for blogging, but for content management of any kind. No matter what kind of website you want to create, I believe that WordPress can do the job for you, and do it well. One of the things that makes WordPress great, in my mind, is that the community of users is so large that there is a vast array of add-on products in the marketplace that will enable you to use WordPress as an effective tool for nearly any website need. The other great thing is that most of these add-on items for WordPress are free. Not all are free, but most are.

When I mention that lots of free resources are available for WordPress, don't take that to mean that I have anything against using software or additions that cost money, I have no problem with that. If the right tool is something that costs money, I will buy it in a heartbeat! In fact, in this e-book, when I tell you how to set up a Membership Site, I am going to advise you to use a piece of software that costs money. Why? Because I believe it is the best tool for the job, without any doubt in my mind. But, in general, when using WordPress, there are usually free tools that rival anything that must be purchased. Just not in every case.

So, in the earlier case study that I told you about, when I was thinking of making my showcase site into a Membership Site, when I was going through the process of doing that, I spent a lot of time studying how to do that, and that is something that I want to share with you in this book. Even though in that case I elected not to go Membership on my site, the research that I did is still valuable and perhaps you can benefit from the knowledge that I gained.

During my search for the right way to set up the Membership aspects of the site, I researched and tried out a number of WordPress Plug-ins for the purpose. A plug-in for WordPress is an additional piece of software that you can easily add to WordPress to enhance the functionality of the website. It is through plug-ins, primarily, that you can really personalize the functionality of your WordPress based site. The combination of different plug-ins is what will personalize your site and make it unique.

In my research into Membership plug-ins for WordPress, the plug-in that I found to be the most functional, with the features that I was looking for is called WP eMember. By using WP eMember, I believe that you can accomplish every task that needs to be done to make your membership site perfect! I use WP eMember on my membership sites, and it works great! The plugin is also very affordable, just $49 to completely get your site up and running!

So what are the features of WP eMember? Well, I am not here to sell you the program, nor do I make money if you buy it, so I am not here to tell you a rundown of every single feature of the plug-in. However, let me just tell you that it is a full featured membership plugin. It is easy to use, and will do everything that you need to do in order to start and operate a membership site using WordPress. You can find the plugin, and full information about it here: https://www.tipsandtricks-hq.com/products Let me also say that if you use the eMember plugin in conjunction with the eStore and WP Affiliate Platform, all available from the same site, you will have a killer Membership site!

I believe that having a Membership site is an excellent way to go. But, I caution you that a membership site should not be done until you have developed a well-known personality on the Internet, built a loyal base of fans and followers, and generally learned about using the Internet to make money. It is a complicated thing to do, and there is no substitute to building a great online persona before going this route. Once you are there, though... this is an excellent path to follow! It works well for me.

# 21 – AFFILIATE MARKETING

Most people who have been making money through the Internet know what Affiliate Marketing is. If you haven't been making money online already, though, you may have no idea what I am talking about!

Affiliate marketing is a way to make money by sending people to make a purchase elsewhere.

Basically, Affiliate Marketing works like this:

You have your own website where people come to read what you have to say, view your photos or whatever. Somebody else (let's call him Joe) has a website where he is selling a product (let's say that he is selling Music CDs). Let's say that your website is about Music, so a lot of your readers are interested in buying CDs.

Joe offers a deal where any people that you send over to his site, if they buy a CD, you get a share of the money. Maybe Joe will give you 10% of the total purchase.

How do you "send somebody over" to Joe's site to make the purchase? Well, you put an advertisement for Joe's site on your site. When your reader clicks on your ad and transfers to Joe's site, the software on Joe's site gets a notification that the buyer came from your site. If that buyer makes a purchase, you get a commission! In most cases, the software on Joe's site sets a "cookie" in the person's browser. With this "cookie" if the buyer goes back a few days later to make the purchase, there is a record that he is "your" customer, and you get the commission. This part of the equation is called "return" time. For example, if the return time is 30 days, if the customer makes any purchases within 30 days of when they clicked the ad on your site, you will get paid a commission. If the customer clicks the ad on your site, but doesn't buy anything, but goes back 2 months later, unfortunately you get nothing.

How do you find Affiliate Programs that you can join and add to your site? Well, that is very, very easy to do! You can join an Affiliate network like "Commission Junction," "ShareASale" and others. All of these networks have literally hundreds, possibly thousands of different companies that are willing to pay Affiliate Commissions for buyers that you send to them.

Many individual companies also have affiliate programs, so you don't have to go through companies like Commission Junction. For example, on my bookstore site, I have an affiliate program. If you want to get into affiliate marketing, go around to websites that sell merchandise that is related to the topic of your website. Look on this sites for affiliate information, and you will find that probably a majority of the sites have an affiliate program that you can join.

I have done Affiliate Marketing over the years, although to be honest, I have only done it half-heartedly in the past. My results have been mixed, but I have been able to consistently earn a couple hundred dollars per month at the times when I have focused a little more on Affiliate Marketing.

That said, I know people who make tens of thousands of dollars per month doing Affiliate Marketing. These people are very focused, and they target their audience with very specific affiliate offerings that produce a lot of income. As I said, I would not consider myself a guru, expert or even that successful at Affiliate Marketing, but I also know for certain that it is something that can be done, if you pay attention, focus, and make a serious effort.

# 22 – GRAPHIC DESIGN BUSINESS

In this book, I have pointed out a lot of different ways that you can make money in the 21st Century.

One business that I believe is particularly lucrative is a graphic design business. Something where you can hire local talent to design graphics for websites, graphics for magazines or advertising. The number of businesses these days who need their own custom graphics are virtually endless. How about people like sign manufacturers, they get a lot of business, and many have teams of designers to come up with the needed graphics. However, it would be much less expensive for a US company to employ only one graphics manager, and to outsource the actual designing work to a place like the Philippines or another developing country.

You can be the person who puts this together! As an expat here, you have access to the customers and also the employees, you are in a perfect position to make it happen. My approach would be to approach companies in the USA (or wherever you came from) and offer your services. You can do it at very good prices, given the low labor costs here, and still make a nice profit for yourself. I mean, if you employ a dozen designers here, you can take a cut from the work that each one does, and come out very good.

So, there are many ways that you can find and line up customers for your service. Start out by looking at your personal friends and acquaintances to see who could use such a service. If you know somebody who owns a sign company, works at an ad agency or operates websites, these are all customers, potentially. You don't have to find too many either, because if you can produce quality work for a handful of people, and at a low price, you can bet that word of mouth is going to carry your name far and wide. You'll find that as time goes on, you will probably be needing to hire additional staff here in the Philippines.

One nice thing is, too, that the talent pool here is very deep, and many people are unemployed or underemployed. This gives you a very large pool of potential employees to select from, and lots of additional resources when you do need to add to your staff.

Here is another thing to consider. In almost each chapter in this book, I am talking about creating your own products, creating your own websites, building websites for clients, that sort of thing. Almost every idea that I lay out in this book can use graphic designers! So, if you get into this business, during down times when you don't have client work, you can be using your design staff to create graphics for your own products and services. This is a natural fit, one where you can use employee down time as productive time for building your own graphic needs!

I believe that the business of Graphic Design is a natural match for here in the Philippines and most other developing countries. And, and expat living here is in a perfect position to take advantage of many angles that can make for a very successful business!

# 23 – FREELANCE JOBS

There are a lot of jobs from overseas that you can do if you have a bit of education, and if you are resourceful. What you are trained in, of course, will influence what jobs you are interested in, and what you are qualified to do. But, there are jobs available in many fields that you can take advantage of.

For example, there are jobs as copywriters, where you would be given a subject and assigned to write about it. Proof-readers are also in demand. If your English skills are adequate, you can get a job as a proof-reader or a copywriter, and make reasonable money, regardless of where in the world you are living.

Basically, you can find jobs like this from many online sources. One source that I like, which includes Blogging jobs as well as these categories as well is the ProBlogger Job Board. However, in addition to that site, there are tons of sites where you can find this kind of work. I have mentioned previously in this book about eLance and other such freelancer websites where jobs are listed, and you'll find this kind of thing there too.

Watch places like Fivrr, Odesk and other freelancer sites where potential employers seek out freelancers to work for them.

One of the prerequisites that you should keep in mind is that if you live in a foreign country you should make sure you have a system in place so that people can pay you! Popular methods of paying or receiving funds would include PayPal, Bank Transfer, 2Checkout, Payoneer and many others. If possible, be able to accept as many of these payment methods as possible, and even more! The easier it is for the employer to get money to you, the less hassle, and the better he will feel about hiring you for his freelance needs. The better chance of people hiring you, the more money you will make.

In these days, it is actually cheaper for many employers to pay a freelancer, even if the price is a bit higher, than to hire you as a regular employee. Hiring an employed can mean that the employer is taking on things like administrative costs, health care costs and governmentally enforced costs if he hires a regular employee. This is great for you - you can charge a bit more, and it will still be less expensive for the employer to use you than hiring a regular employee. Also, it frees you up to work for multiple people at the same time, since you are not permanently committed to a single employer. This sort of arrangement is, I believe, the way it will be in years to come! So, get an early start at the lifestyle of the future by doing freelance work now! It will put you steps ahead of the competition!

# SECTION 4 - ONLINE LEARNING

Online learning is a wave that you need to catch for the future.

# 24 – ONLINE TEACHING

Are you familiar with Udemy? Udemy.com. Udemy is the mammoth in the field of Online Education. It is not any kind of online university or high school, it is a site where anybody can teach a course, and make money doing it.

For me, I discovered Udemy about a year ago. Maybe a year and a half. I first just studied it to see what people were doing there. After a few weeks, I decided that I should take advantage of the opportunities that Udemy offered to me.

I started thinking about what I could teach that would have some demand, and also that I had adequate knowledge about to actually teach a course.

Back in 2007, I took classes in the Cebuano language. I graduated the class (a live one-on-one class with a tutor, not an online course) in 2011. So, Cebuano is my second language, and I can do pretty well with it. Cebuano is a language that is used in the southern half of the Philippines. Because I have a large following of readers and friends who are interested in living in the Philippines, I decided that maybe I should teach the Cebuano language.

When I looked into this possibility, I found that Udemy had no courses in the Cebuano language! There are courses for dozens of languages on Udemy, but none for Cebuano. I have a Kindle book called "Survival Cebuano" and it is one of my best selling Kindle books, so that shows me that there is demand for resources to learn how to speak Cebuano.

A few months earlier, I had started building my own membership site for teaching a complete Cebuano course online. As I thought about it, I felt that Udemy would be an excellent platform for selling a sort of "conversational Cebuano" course, aimed at travelers rather than people who lived in the Philippines. Something where people could learn basics, phrases and basically just enough Cebuano to get by on the streets of the Philippines. I decided to call the course "Survival Cebuano" and be a companion to the book that I had on the Kindle platform.

I started looking into how to produce a course for Udemy, and frankly it was very easy. In fact, when you sign up to be an instructor on Udemy you will be given a full course that will teach you how to produce a course. It will tell you the rules, and give tips on how to be successful. Udemy wants your course to be successful, because that is how they make money from it. If nobody buys your course, Udemy makes nothing (same as you!), and there is no incentive for that. So, they want to teach you ho to succeed.

When you register to become an instructor on Udemy, you will receive an invitation to join a group on Facebook that is operated by Udemy. When you join this group you will be able to interact with other instructors, and with Udemy staff. The only people who are allowed into this closed group are instructors and Udemy staff. Through this group you can exchange a lot of information with other instructors and learn new tricks and tips for what works, and what doesn't.

In addition to the Udemy sponsored Facebook group, there are many other groups on Facebook for Udemy instructors. One advantage of these other groups is that instructors will post coupon codes online so that you can take their course for free. I have literally taken dozens of Udemy courses for free, some of these courses cost hundreds of dollars to join if you don't have the coupon. By taking these courses you can see what other instructors are doing with their courses - good or bad. If you see good things, you can incorporate those teaching styles into your own course. If you see bad things then you know things to avoid in your course.

It took me about 2 months to complete my Udemy course. After finishing it, though, I know that I could have done it in 2 weeks or less if I just kept my nose to the grindstone. I worried too much about making mistakes and such instead of just getting it done.

While teaching the Cebuano language is a very, very tiny niche, my course does make money. While some people make thousands of dollars each month on Udemy, my course makes me anywhere from $100 to $300 in a month, which is fine. I knew that it would not be a course that would earn thousands. When I did the Cebuano course, I looked at it as more of a learning experience for me to learn how to do a Udemy course, so that at a later time I could produce courses that had larger earning potential.

One good thing about Udemy is that they do not claim exclusive rights to your course. So, you can produce a course for Udemy, put it up on their site and start making money. Then, you can take that same course and put it up on your own website, and charge an access fee there as well, which is what I do.

I will caution you on pricing with Udemy. When you read about Udemy you will learn that there are different revenue sharing percentages. But, Udemy does not emphasize just how little you might make. I am OK with the way they do it, but I was a bit surprised when I started seeing how little I was earning from the courses.

For example, my Survival Cebuano course is $29, that is the "list price" of the course. If I put up an ad on my site and people click through directly from my site, I get nearly 100% of the revenue. Udemy keeps a very small amount, 3%, to cover their costs of delivering the course. So, out of $29, I would make about $28. If somebody goes to the Udemy website and searches and finds my course, I get less. In that case, I would get 50% and Udemy gets 50%. That seems fair to me. So, I would get nearly $15 in that case.

Next, you have to consider that Udemy has an affiliate program, where people can advertise Udemy on their own websites. If somebody clicks on an affiliate banner to get to Udemy, then that affiliate gets 50% of the sale. So, if that is the route that a student takes to Udemy, and they buy my $29 course, the affiliate would get 50%, Udemy would get 25% and I would get 25%. In that case I would get $7.50 or so for an affiliate initiated sale of my course. $7.50 out of $29, it is getting smaller and smaller.

But, the kicker is that Udemy will have sales on the courses. They do not ask you if a certain price is OK or anything like that, they just set the price. And, when Udemy has a sale, they really lower the price! So, Udemy will often offer my $29 course for a sale price of $10, this is very common. So, if they offer the course for $10, I could get $9+ for the course if the student came in through my own promotion on my website. I could get $5 if the student came directly to the Udemy website organically. Or, if the sale came from a Udemy affiliate, I would get only $2.50 for my $29 course. Well, for $2.50, is it really worth it? Probably not.

However, while that was pretty shocking at first, and I didn't like it, I have resolved it in my own mind, and I am OK with it. I just figure that the $2.50 that I got for that sale is $2.50 that I otherwise would not have gotten at all.

When you sign up to be an instructor for Udemy, you are given the option to not participate in promotions, though. So, Udemy will not put your course on sale. My experience, though, is that I get a ton of course sales through the promotions that Udemy offers, so I would still go ahead and participate in the promotions program at Udemy. The more people that take the course, even at a very low price, can lead to more sales through word of mouth and such. Also, that student may go on and take my full Cebuano course on my own website if they liked my Udemy teaching, and that course is $200, so even a $2.50 sale on Udemy could potentially lead to a nice sale down the road for me.

I started my Udemy course in January of 2015. At the time of this writing in July 2015, I have had around 400 students who have taken the course so far, so I consider that to be a success. As I mentioned earlier in this chapter, I do plan to offer additional courses on Udemy, which shows that I have been happy overall with the results.

# 25 – OFFER COURSES ON YOUR OWN SITE

As I pointed out previously, Online Education is a real wave of the future. There are some great opportunities in this area, and you can get in now on the ground floor.

College is getting so expensive, and student debt is finally being pointed to as a flawed system, so I firmly believe that it will become more common for people to take highly targeted online courses to supplement their education so that they can learn the things needed for their work, or the work that they wish to do. The days of borrowing tens of thousands of dollars to attend college are going to change drastically. It is too expensive, and leaves the student in great debt.

So, you can use your expertise to teach others in the area on which you hold that expertise. Udemy is one of the premier online education websites, and you can use it to reach a very broad audience of potential earners.

I pointed out in my chapter about teaching on Udemy, though, that the various fees involved on Udemy can really eat into your earnings when you sell on Udemy. For example, I have a course there which is $29, and often the amount I make when a student enrolls in my course is as low a $2.50. Not much to get excited about.

But, the great thing is that Udemy does not take exclusive rights to market your course when you teach there. Since you must prepare an entire course before you can teach on Udemy, why not take that same course and sell it to your own audience on your website? That is what I do, and it works great. When I sell the course on my own site, I always get the full $29 for myself, less a small amount that PayPal charges for processing the payment. I have to sell more than 10 courses on Udemy to get the same amount that I get when I sell just one course on my own site!

In another chapter of this book, I talk about "Multi-tasking" your products. Use the same product over and over again in different ways. It gives you an opportunity to make money from the same work that you did, and make that money many times over. If you make a course and sell it on Udemy and nothing else, you are walking away from money.

Be careful about one thing, though. Under Udemy's rules, you must not give away the course for free, and you cannot sell it for less than Udemy is selling for. I have no problem with that at all, I like to make money, and I have no interest in giving my products away.

How do you know what to teach? Maybe you have expertise on a broad area of interest, but knowing EXACTLY what to teach might be a tough choice. I have figured out a way to know exactly what to teach, exactly what books to write, etc. How do I do it? I let my readers and customers tell me what they want!

How do you get your readers to tell you what they want? It is not hard. You just read the emails that they send you. If you get the same questions over and over again, which would be very common, those questions are the ones that you need to answer. Use that information to know what to write about or what to teach about.

**The mechanics**

When you want to teach a course on your own website, the recommended way of doing this would be by setting up a WordPress site (that is the platform that I use and recommend) and a membership plugin. By doing this, you can charge people money in order to be a "member" of each course that you teach. You can set different prices for each membership level, or course on your site. For information on how to set this all up, check the chapter in this book about setting up a membership website.

# SECTION 5 – SOFTWARE

Using programming skills to make money.

# 26 – CREATE WEBSITE TEMPLATES

One area that is quickly growing is the business for Website Templates or Themes. There is a thriving market for website designs that people can buy and use to create their own sites. Prices on such designs range from about $50 or so for rather simple designs that will be sold multiple times, up to Thousands of Dollars for more complex designs that will be sold on an exclusive basis.

One of the best ways to get into this business, too, is to simply create some free designs to "show off" your skills. As your designs get downloaded and used by more people, you will start gaining a reputation based on the work that you are offering. As your reputation grows your designs will increase in worth, and also attract more people who are willing to pay for your designs.

Another good thing about creating a bunch of free templates is that the more templates you make, the more your skills will improve. Your sense of design will improve. Watch and see which designs are getting downloaded the most, and that will tell you what is popular. You can deduce design features that people like the most, and that will help you know how to design the premium templates that you will charge money for.

If you offer the templates for unlimited downloads, you can expect to get prices from $50 up to $300 or even $400 for your designs. People will understand that the particular design might be purchased hundreds, even thousands of times, thus they may find other sites using the exact same design that they have.

Alternatively, you can choose some of your designs to sell exclusively, or to a limited number of customers. For example, you might say that a certain design will be taken off the market once it has sold to ten different people. Or, you might say that it will be retired after one purchase. The more exclusive you make the design, the higher the price that you will be able to get for it.

You will find that there are people selling their website designs like this on eBay, and through other marketplaces too. Additionally, there are entire websites devoted to selling such themes and designs.

Offering various Website Templates can pay off big for you!

How do you decide what kinds of designs to make? Well, firstly, you need to design themes that work with certain software packages. For example,

WordPress is the most popular blogging software in the world today, and there are literally millions of people using WordPress for their blogs. Alternatively, there are other blogging platforms that are much smaller with only hundreds or a few thousand people using the software for their sites. If you design a theme that works with WordPress, your potential market is huge compared to the others. Alternatively, if you find a niche market with one of the other platforms, you might find that you have little or no competition in that field.

And, there is demand for lots of designs other than for blogs. How about e-Commerce designs for OSCommerce? Basically, any e-Commerce platform can use templates in one way or another, and you can make money by designing such templates. Another big ecommerce platform is Magento, you could design templates for that as well. Study what software platforms people are using for various types of websites, and design what the market is demanding!

Another way to make additional money in this same field is to sell not only the templates and themes, but also offer installation. Many people don't know how to install such things, or are afraid to try, because they don't want to mess up their site. If you can install the theme for them, you can make up to $200 or so just to do a quick installation and make sure that everything is working!

Doing this installation will likely also help you sell more templates! If a person is not tech savvy but wants a new theme for his website, he is much more likely to choose your theme if you offer an installation service for him, even if he has to pay for it. Fear of messing up your site is a huge motivator. A non-geek can have an ecommerce site that is making money for him. If he tries to do things to the site which are beyond his technical skills, and his attempt takes his site offline, he could lose thousands of dollars in sales! It could take him many days to fix the problem that he created himself. Thus, it would be less expensive for him in the long run if he just pays you $200 or even $500 to install the theme and give his site a new look. That will make more money for you. In fact, you may find that you can make money by simply offering installation of such themes or templates, even if you did not do the design! If a person buys a theme from another designer, there is no reason that you cannot do the installation!

Some entrepreneurs are really capitalizing on this demand by offering some really special designs. One person that I follow in the field of WordPress themes is Michael Pollock of Solostream Studios. Actually, Michael has since retired from this field, but he was a pioneer in doing premium WordPress themes for sale.

If you take a look at Michael's former website (SoloStream.com) you will see that he combines many different things into a single site. He has a blog where he can talk about entrepreneurial things, talk about his theme designs and such. He also has his sales site for selling his themes. He used to offer free theme downloads, but as time has passed, Michael has gained enough reputation that he no longer needs to offer freebies to attract people – he is already well known enough that he gets enough paying customers.

One thing that is interesting with the way that Michael is selling his work, though, is that he is using a tiered pricing system, just as I have recommended above. For example, for one of his themes, you have three different options when you buy:

You can flat out buy the theme for $79. With this option, you can use the theme on one website only, and you may not modify the theme footer, which includes links back to Michael.

You can purchase a multiple-use license for $179, which allows you to use the theme on as many of your own sites as you wish. and you may also modify the footer links (including removing them). So, for an extra $100, you can use the theme over and over again, as long as they are on your own sites. For $279 (another $100 for Michael) you can buy a Theme Developer license. Under this license, you can actually make derivative works and re-sell them yourself! You can even make websites using the theme, and sell the websites.

Now, see what I mean about tiered pricing? I particularly like option #3, because you can actually make some changes the theme, then re-brand it and sell it yourself! If you do that, you would not even have to hire a team of designers, as I have suggested.

Basically, along the lines of this business idea that I have suggested, a really nice business model would be to simply buy up themes under a developer's license, make modifications (maybe offer the same theme with different color schemes, that is an easy change to make) and then start up your own theme store online. It doesn't get much simpler than that!

And, don't be scared if you don't know how to design websites! As I have said elsewhere in this book, you don't have to know, you can hire local talent to do the work! The more you know, the better, but you can also learn as you go along.

# 27 – APP DEVELOPMENT

Are you reading this book right now? There is an app for that, you know? I am just kidding.. as far as I know there is no app (yet) that will read for you! But, it is a common thing these days that there is an app that will do just about anything you need to have done!

Whether it be for an Android Phone, iPhone, any kind of tablet, or a desktop PC, there are Apps for everything now, it seems.

Guess what? Somebody had to develop all of those apps! They didn't just appear by themselves.

Have you ever thought of learning how to develop apps? I am not a developer, but I know plenty of people who are doing this. I am told that it is not too difficult to do. Maybe you are a 74 year old grandmother, though, who has vision problems and doesn't know how to type. That's not a problem, you can still develop apps! As I have mentioned elsewhere in this book, even if you don't know how to do something you can easily hire a team of people who do know how to do it! And, these days you can usually do that inexpensively.

Many of us have become conditioned to the notion that outsourcing is a bad thing. If you have been working a job for the past 20 years and you suddenly get laid off from your work because the company is sending your job to some outsourcing center in China, well, I can understand why you might have hard feelings about outsourcing.

But, if you are that 74 year old granny that I mentioned, and you can hire a team of 20 computer programmers to develop and app that will make good money for you, and it will only cost you $500 to get the team that you need... well.. outsourcing may not be the big negative that you previously thought!

How many times have you been doing some mundane task and you thought to yourself... "if only there was an app to do this.." Well, there can be! If you have a killer idea that a lot of people would want to do, an app may be your key to riches. Truth is, not every app developer is a multi-millionaire, but there are certainly a lot of app developers who have earned a very nice sum of money, and you can be the next one on the list. Even if you don't know how to do it! Really, all you have to know is what you want the app to do, and how to find a team of developers who can help you solve the problem!

The problem? Yep. Every business, every app needs to solve some problem!

That is how business works. You may be thinking.. what problem does a grocery store solve? Well, it solves the problem that you are hungry! What problem does a library solve? It solves the problem that you need information.

So, if you have some kind of problem, think of a way that an app could fix the problem. Once you know what the problem is and how an app could correct the problem, start developing the app, or searching for the developers that you need to hire to make the app.

Apps are the wave of the future. Jump on the wave now.. you can still get in on the ground floor!

# SECTION 6 - GENERAL

General ideas that will keep you earning.

# 28 – MULTI-TASK YOUR PRODUCTS

There is a key word in the title of this chapter. Products. I have said previously in this book, but perhaps I have not emphasized it enough, I believe that the key to success in the 21st Century is to have products of your own.

Through blogging and other online activity you can make yourself known and develop a following. If you do it right you can develop a significant number of followers. These are the people that will buy your products. Out of your following, you will have some super fans. These super fans will buy every item that you put on the market.

There are other ways to make money too. You can go with PPC advertising. You can sell other people's products through an affiliate program. So many ways, but I firmly believe that there is no better method to make money in the 21st Century than making and selling your own products.

When you sell your own products, in many cases you get to keep nearly 100% of the sale price. If you are selling on your own website, and selling some kind of electronic/digital product, then the only cut to come out of your selling price is that PayPal or some other payment processor will charge you, which generally ranges from around 2% up to a maximum of around 5%.

On the other hand, if you sell your products through some kind of service like Amazon, eBay, etc., there will be fees to pay and in some cases a percentage of the profit to share with the vendor who sells the item for you. Because of these factors, I believe that it is always best and most desirable to sell your products through your own website. However, there is an exception. Companies like Amazon and eBay have huge amounts of web traffic. They are the elephants in the world of ecommerce. If you have followed the recommendations that I have laid out in this book, you should be building a good following of your own. But, no matter how hard you try, it is unlikely that you will ever develop a web following anywhere near the number of people that visit eBay or Amazon on a regular basis. Because of this, even if you have to give up a percentage of the earnings to sell on Amazon or elsewhere, the advantage is that you can sell much larger quantities of merchandise if you are willing to take a bit less of the amount of money generated.

For me, this is a no-brainer. Taking a smaller piece of a much larger pie is always an advantage. Truth is, you can still sell your products on your own website, but selling at a place like Amazon in addition to your site will bring you sales to a lot of people who don't even know who you are. Your followers and fans will still go to your site, and the vast majority of them will still buy from your site. You will get very close to 100% of the money generated for those sales. However, people who mostly would have never purchased your product in the first place will find your offering on Amazon, or elsewhere, and many will buy it. Yes, you will get maybe only half as much money, but you will also sell a multiple of the numbers of items that would have been sold on your own site. It is a no-lose situation if you ask me.

Now, what do I mean with the title of this chapter? "Multitasking" your products? Part of what I mean was spelled out in the last couple of paragraphs. Get more out of your own products by selling the products via multiple channels. Sell your item on your own website. Sell it on eBay. Sell it on Amazon. Sell it every way you can possibly think of.

But, multitasking goes beyond that! Way beyond that. Use the same product in different ways at the same time. For example, the book that you are reading right now. Even as I am still writing it, I am thinking about marketing methods that will be pulled into play when the book is ready. Traditionally, I would have written the book, formatted it as an eBook and put it up for sale. I would then move on to another product. Well, I am still going to move on to another product, but in a little different way. I will finish writing this book and make it into an eBook. I will also create another new product, a paperback version of this book. I will also create an online course based on this book with a little more in-depth information on each of the ways to make a living that I am laying out in this book. After creating my online course, I will put the entire course on a set of CDs and have a CD fulfillment house in the USA press the disks and they will also be my fulfillment provider to ship the disks wherever I need to send them. I will sell the courses on eBay and on Amazon using their FBA program. I will the course disks on my own website and have the CD fulfillment company ship the disks to the people who purchase the course on CD.

So, as you can see, this product will be multitasking in many different ways once it is completed!

But wait! There is even more. If you tend to write about similar topics over and over, and we all do that to some extent, you can repurpose the content over and over again.

Why would you write on the same topic over and over again? Well, it is your niche. It is your area of expertise. It is the topic that people know you for. Zig Zigler writes about self-help type topics. Stephen King writes horror books. There are popular writers in every niche. You probably would not go to the bookstore looking for the latest horror novel by Zig Zigler, right?

So, based on the fact that it is normal to have a niche that you write about, it is likely that you will write many books (if you are a writer) on the topic of your niche, what people know you for. Myself, I write many books about living in the Philippines, and about business topics. Those two topics are highly interesting to me, I feel that I know a fair amount about each topic, and people know me for those topics, so they look for what I have to offer them.

So, if you write a book about writing eBooks and it is a good seller, you have just gotten a clue that the book has good information in it. If it was not good, people would not be buying it so often. Later, if you write a book about how to make money on the Internet, you will probably want to include a section about writing eBooks. Since you have this very popular eBook on that topic already, you can likely include some of that same information in your new book. I don't mean to copy the whole thing over, that would not be fair to the people who buy both books. But, you can include the ideas. You can (and should) also update the information to include the latest trends and information on the topic in the newer book. That gives great value even to those who bought the earlier book, and purchase the later book as well, because you will be updating them with fresh information that they need to know.

There are many ways to put your products to work for you in multiple ways. This is something that is very important in helping you publish a lot of great information quickly and in different ways that attract a larger audience. You will find, if you look into it, that different people learn and digest information in different ways. Some people learn best by reading. For those people your books will be a great solution. Other people learn best by hearing the information, so something like an audiobook would be great to provide the information to those people. Still other people learn best with one on one teaching... something like a video course, or even one-on-one personal consulting is best for that person. If you provide the same information in multiple different media, you will capture a much larger audience.

# 29 – FRANCHISING

Firstly, you can buy a franchise! It might not be as expensive as you think it is.

Anytime that you open up a new business, the chances of failure are there. Some would even say that failure is the most probable outcome, and given the statistics, they are probably right. Most new businesses end in failure (thankfully, that has not been true for me, but it is for most new businesses). However, one way to battle that is by opening a Franchise.

What is a Franchise? Well, it is when you purchase the right to open a new branch of an existing successful business. For example, McDonald's is a franchise business. Most McDonald's stores are not owned by the company, but rather have been franchised out to individual business men around the world. McDonald's, of course, keeps very tight control over how the businesses are run – they must mostly all be the exact same in terms of what they sell, how the food tastes, etc. It is because of this company control that when a new McDonald's franchise opens, it is very likely to succeed. Think about this – how many McDonald's have you seen open up and then close down because they didn't do well? Not many, if any at all. On the other hand, how many times have you seen a new unknown burger stand open up and go out of business in a few months? It happens all the time.

Now, if you want to open a McDonald's or another big name franchise business, you need a lot of money. Just getting the franchise will cost millions. On top of that, you have to buy the items needed to run the place. You'll spend several Million dollars to get started, in my estimation. Most of us don't have that kind of money available - I know that I don't.

However, the good news is that you can open a Franchise in many parts of the world for a smaller company very reasonably. For $10,000 or so, you can get a good business started. This won't apply to Americans, but for many parts of the world it is very true.

For somebody who is less entrepreneurial, and less experienced in business, a Franchise is a great way to go, because you will be fully trained by the Franchisor on how to operate the business, and how to make it successful. If you don't succeed, it makes the Franchisor look bad, and makes it hard for them to sell additional units of the franchise, so training is very important, and your success is vital to the Franchisor! Because of this, your chances of success are very high, provided that you pay attention to the training!

Secondly, you can start your own business, then offer it as a franchise!

If you come up with a successful business, why not offer franchises to others? Offering a franchise of your operation can offer benefits for you as well as others.

The benefit for others is that they get to come into a business that has already proven successful, has established some recognition in it's field, and has a formula for success!

The benefit for you is that you can establish your business in new areas where you don't have a presence, and without any additional outlay of capital, you can make money from the expansion.

There basically are two ways you make money from franchising. First, the customer will pay a franchise fee to you for the right to open a copy of your business in their location. Secondly, you will get residual payments from the customer over the long haul. Every franchise agreement is different, but usually the franchisee will pay a percentage of sales or profits to the franchisor. Or, perhaps you will supply the raw materials to the franchisee, making your profits from marking these raw materials up.

The nice thing about franchising for you (the franchisor) is that you can maintain complete control over how the business is operated, even though you don't have to put up any of the money. Think of it like this – no matter where you go in the world, if you see a McDonald's, it generally has the same look to it. They don't put up "red arches" in China – the arches are golden no matter where on the earth you are located. And, the menu, while it may have slight regional variation, will include basically the same food items worldwide. Here in the Philippines, McDonald's has chicken and rice, but they also still sport the famous hamburgers, Quarter Pounders and Big Macs that you find worldwide. So, although McDonald's Corporation doesn't own these franchised outlets, the outlets must operate strictly the way that McDonald's tells them. If they try to change it in an unapproved way, they will lose the franchise!

This is attractive to a businessman (like you or me) because we can then ensure that the business franchise is maintaining our quality standards, and representing us well, no matter where they are located. And, on top of that, you make money from their operation! What could be better?

I have a friend, Rudolf Kotik, who is in the franchise business here in the Philippines. Rudolf is originally from Austria, but has been living here in the Philippines for nearly 3 decades now. Rudolf has worked in the franchising industry for many years now, and worked for franchise giants, including McDonalds in the past. So, he knows his business when it comes to franchising.

If you want to get into franchising, you need to first start a business, make it successful, and operate for a minimum of one year before you consider franchising it. Why a full year? Well, for several reasons. First, you want to make sure that the business succeeds over the long haul. If you do well your first month, you are not yet ready to franchise until you see if you can maintain that level of success. Another factor is that many businesses are very seasonal. For example, if you opened up a costume shop, and your grand opening is in October, you will probably have a super month for that first month, because Halloween is October 31, and there is a great demand for costumes in October. However, in later months you may find that your business is not doing as well.

Because of the seasonality of businesses, it is good to make it through an entire calendar year to see how things go through each and every season, before trying to sell the franchise to others.

I have personally been involved in franchising from both ends of the business during my life in the Philippines. I have owned a business that I franchised, and I have also purchased a franchise as well.

Purchasing a franchise did not work out well for me. Why? Because if you buy a franchise, you MUST follow the rules laid out by the Franchisor. If you cannot do that, you will not be a successful franchisee. My problem is that I don't like following what other people tell me. I am the type who comes up with ideas on how to make improvements, and that is what I want to do. If I bought a McDonald's, though, and put up Red Arches, and changed the menu to Italian food, you can bet that my franchise would not last for long!

So, if you intend to buy a franchise, make sure that you are of the personality type who can follow directions! That is just not for me, I am more entrepreneurial, and that doesn't work.

If you develop a business and start selling franchises, though, you are free to experiment, and even impose those improvements in the business system on your franchisees. That is the end of franchising that is more interesting for me. But, we are all of different personalities, and you need to decide which end of the business would be best for you.

When I say franchising, many people think of millions of dollars and such, like if you buy a franchise of a McDonald's restaurant, indeed, you need really deep pockets. The franchise game in the Philippines, and other smaller countries, though, is not as difficult to enter. Here, if you have a budget of even $10,000 or so, you can buy a franchise. If you are selling a franchise, don't look for huge money up front – it's better to make your money over the long term relationship with your franchisee.

If you have a business that you want to franchise, I strongly recommend getting a consultant to assist you with the process. Somebody like my friend Rudolf helps develop a business to successfully franchise itself. Rudolf tells me, and I agree 100%, that those who try to develop their business for franchising themselves are fools. For Rudolf, he charges at least a double fee to those who try to do it themselves and fail. Why charge more to consult those who have failed? Because generally, they have created a mess which must be cleaned up before moving forward in the proper way. Do yourself a favor, and hire a professional from the start – you won't be sorry.

# 30 - CONSULTING

As I have said in other parts of this book, we all have at least one area of expertise! Another way that you can put your expertise to work is by consulting.

I have a friend who is also an expat here in the Philippines who has done consulting work several times now. This fellow has an extensive background in many different businesses in the UK before moving to the Philippines. Somebody like this person can put his business expertise to work by consulting local companies to help them improve their business practices and end up making better money because of the consulting.

The fact is, whether it is true or not, a lot of Filipinos believe that foreigners have more knowledge on business matters than they do. Foreigners are looked at more as experts. Personally, I don't necessarily believe that this is correct, but it is a fact that a lot of Filipinos think this way.

I believe that with this kind of attitude out there, money can be made by doing something like consulting. Consulting basically means that you would go into the business, observe how things are being done, and help them improve their way of doing business. As a result of making these improvements, the local business would be looking to earn more money either by garnering more business, improving their profit margin, or both.

When my friend did his first consulting job, I visited the business early on, and I saw a lot of opportunities for improvement. There were basically no customers there on my first visit. By the time that my friend completed his consulting (maybe 6 or 7 months in all), there were so many customers that I could not find an empty place in the Parking Lot!

My friend made money, the business learned how to make more profit, the customers seemed to enjoy the improvements. It was a winner all around. And, within weeks my friend had been hired to do consulting for another company.

In my example with my British friend, he was living in the Philippines and brought his British know-how to a local business. But, don't forget that in today's world with the Internet you can go way beyond that. With services like Skype, Viber or other VOIP services you can now consult worldwide without leaving the comfort of your home or office. I recently put together a team of experts to consult with people who want to live in the Philippines. I assembled a team of 6 people from foreign countries who have all lived long term in the Philippines and we have a consulting website where we can advise people who wish to make the move themselves.

This service that we recently put together is just an example of what you could do. No matter if you live in Iowa City, London or Prague, if you have expertise you can consult a person in Tokyo, Beijing or New Delhi. Location is just not a concern these days because of technology. So, think about where your expertise lies, brush up on that expertise if you need to, and then start offering your services. You might be surprised at how much consulting business you can do!

If you have some kind of business expertise that you bring with you to the Philippines, why not consider doing some consulting, and make a little money from your knowledge?

# 31 – TEACH ENGLISH

These days, with so many world economies interconnected, there is a real need to be able to speak English. You, as a native English speaker can profit from that. People from just about every country have a need to be able to speak English these days. It is the only way that people can be competitive in the job market these days.

Here in the Philippines, where I live, there are people from other Asian countries who come to the Philippines specifically to learn how to speak English. Since the Philippines is an English speaking country, people from other countries in the region can come here and take advantage of the relatively inexpensive cost of labor, hire an English teacher and live a nice life while learning to speak English.

Additionally, there are people from all over the world who hire Filipinos (and foreigners living in the Philippines) to teach them conversational English via Skype or another VOIP service. In fact I know a number of Americans who are retired here in the Philippines, but they teach conversational English via Skype to earn extra income.

For a Korean who wants to learn English, it would be much more preferable to learn it from a native English speaker like a British, American or Australian than from a Filipino. Thus, you can really capitalize on this, and make a nice amount of money in this field.

In the Philippines, some people who are in the language training business offer a full service operation. They have like a boarding house where the student can stay, offer meals, language tutoring and everything. With all of these services at your disposal, you can turn a very nice profit on the business.

I basically see a couple of different avenues that you could follow in this business. As I mentioned above, a lot of Koreans come to the Philippines to learn English (and other nationalities too), so this is the most obvious avenue.

The second avenue for success is a young market that is growing rapidly. As you probably know, Outsourcing of things like Call Centers is becoming a big business in many locations around the world. One of the biggest problems in this business is finding people with good English skills to be call center agents. A Call Center agent will basically spend his working hours on the telephone, talking with clients in the USA (or another country, but primarily US clients). Because of this, the agent needs to possess very good

English skills. In fact, he must speak "American English" if he is dealing with US clients, so that they can fully communicate with each other.

This is where you can come in. You can teach Filipinos better English skills, American phrases and such. You know these things, you just need to build a curriculum of this so that you can teach it to local people who want to succeed in the Call Center business.

In the past 15 years or so, a lot of foreigners have gotten into this kind of business, and many have made very good money at it too. In my opinion, if you feel that you can be a good language teacher, this is one type of business that you really should look at hard. Over the past decade or so, watching people get into this English teaching, it really has proven this as a good field to get into. This would probably not be big enough to be a job replacer, but if you are retired, or just need some supplemental income, this is an excellent way to do it. Low stress, a fairly good wage level, and plenty of potential clients out there looking for a good teacher. If you are from an English speaking country, this is an excellent way to go.

# 32 – DO A NEWSLETTER

If you are blogging, that should mean two things:

1.  You have some area of expertise that you are blogging about.

2.  You have some people reading your site, especially if you have already been blogging for some time.

With these two items in place, maybe it's time for you to take the next step and start publishing a newsletter to accompany your blog.

There are a couple of choices when it comes to your newsletter. First, you could do an electronic version that you e-mail out to all of your subscribers. If you do an electronic newsletter, it is harder to charge money for it, although some people are able to succeed in the paid newsletter market. Another option you could consider is to put paid advertising in your newsletter. Truth is, though, my experience is that even if I don't charge a subscription fee, whenever I send out a newsletter, I generally make money from it. That is because I advertise my products in my newsletter. I would not recommend sending out a "newsletter" that is nothing but ads, but rather make the main part of your newsletter a really meaty read with lots of information. For an added touch advertise the products that you offer. I always advertise my books in my newsletter. I sent out a newsletter about 5 days ago, and each day since sending out the newsletter I have sold between $80 to $125 worth of books. These are sales that came directly from the newsletter. So, the newspaper produced significant income for me.

The second possibility would be to publish an actual paper newsletter that will be mailed out to subscribers. Even just a 3 or 4 page newsletter that is sent out monthly can be valuable. I have a friend who lives in California, and he publishes a rather small legal newsletter, and charges more than $1,000 per year for a subscription – the information in the newsletter is that valuable. While you may not come up with a newsletter that is worth $1,000 per year, it is likely that you could come up with something that might bring $49 to $200 or so per year, if you are a good writer and can offer important information.

It is important that you do not publish the same information in your newsletter that can be found on your blog, otherwise, why would anybody subscribe? One thing you can do is to use your blog as a "teaser" by offering some information on certain topics, with the details on the topic available in your newsletter.

Even if you don't require people to pay for the newsletter, you can still make money by offering the newsletter. How? By using the names and e-mail addresses to build a list of potential clients for upcoming product launches and such. I am not recommending that you sell your mailing list to others, a lot of your clients won't like that. But, if somebody is subscribing to your newsletter about trampolines, and in 6 months you come out with a book about the best Trampoline Construction Tips, you bet that your newsletter subscriber will want to hear about that! So, build a list, and don't just let it sit dormant – profit from it!

I use MailChimp for mailing out my various Newsletters. A company like MailChimp sends out the emails for my Newsletters. They are of great service, because they get the emails delivered. If you sent out mass email like that using your own email account, the majority of the emails you sent would end up in the Spam folder of the recipient, in other words it would be worthless.

I have a number of different newsletters, on different topics, for different blogs. My main Newsletter, the "biggie" is my "MindanaoBob Newsletter" which primarily focuses on moving to or living in the Philippines. That particular mailing list runs about 1800 subscribers. My other Newsletters, about 5 others, range from just 5 subscribers up to 65 subscribers.

On MailChimp, I have the "Forever Free" account. As the name implies, it is free, no charge. However, there are limitations. For a Forever Free account, MailChimp allows you up to a total of 2,000 subscribers. Also, for each month you can send out a total of 12,000 emails. So, for example, if you have 2,000 subscribers, and sent out emails to your entire subscriber list, you could send out 6 emails per month, and no more, unless you step up to a paid account.

At this time, i am fine using the free account, but in time I may start paying, if the need arises. The reason why I have never bothered with a paid account is because I have not been good about sending out Newsletters. Yesterday, I decided that I needed to send one out, so I went to MailChimp and looked at my account. The last time I sent out a Newsletter was around 6 months ago, or so. Boom.. I immediately found out that I suddenly had more than 2,000 subscribers! Just a little bit over. So, if I wanted to send out an email, I needed to upgrade my account.

**What did I do?**

The first thing I did was go to my mailing list subscribers and pruned it down. I deleted people. How did I know who to delete? Well, I didn't need to delete very many to get under the limit, so I started looking for duplication. I found a number of people who had subscribed under multiple email addresses. I deleted any email addresses above one for those people. Next, I found some spammer types who had subscribed (under known spam domains from Russia and such). Frankly, it was pretty easy to get below 2,000 subscribers.

## Why not just go for a paid account?

Well, I might go for a paid account, but this was not the time. Why? Because I had not sent out a newsletter for so long! I will explain that shortly.

You see, if you sent out a mass email like this, some of the emails will bounce because people closed that email account. Also, some people are no longer interested in getting those emails from you, so when they get your Newsletter they will unsubscribe. So, once I pruned my list and sent out an email, boom... like 65 emails bounced, so that reduced my list by 65 more emails. Next, so far, 9 people unsubscribed from the list. They just were no longer interested. If somebody is not interested any longer, I want them to unsubscribe. If they are not interested, they really are not a good prospect for sales or even reading of what I write to them, so unsubscribing is fine. Not only does it stop from bothering the person, it also gives me more room on my list for subscribers who want those emails!

Another thing.... if you send out an email and the person thinks that it is Spam, they may report it as Spam. If you get too many Spam reports, then companies like MailChimp will ban you from using their company for sending out bulk emails. So, if you don't send out a Newsletter for a LONG time, many people will forget that they singed up for your Newsletter, and they think that it is Spam. It is not Spam, because they signed up, and said that they wanted it. Spam is unsolicited email, and they certainly did ask to get this.

So, sending out emails on a regular basis is a way to keep your list fresh, and people know and remember that they are the ones who signed up to receive the emails. Sending out the mail regularly keeps your list fresh. That is why I wanted to prune down my list, both through manual pruning and natural attrition, before paying to keep the extra subscribers.

Now, I have things set up where I will be sending out weekly emails to my subscribers. By doing that, I can then keep my list fresh at all times. If I now get too many subscribers, I will feel fine about paying for the service!

# 33 – MUNDANE COMPUTER JOBS

You can make money from doing mundane things, in fact you can make a mint! You know why? Because things that are quite mundane to you may seem quite complex to others. What you think is simple and boring may in fact be quite difficult for the majority of people!

I have made some really serious money over the years taking on jobs that I can easily do on the computer, that others were doing manually. When I showed them what I could do for them, they gladly paid me in order to rid themselves of a mundane manual job.

The first time that I did something like this, it was in the late 80's. I found where somebody was publishing a book with information, somewhat similar to a phone book, except the information given was a location. I thought about it, and decided that instead of a list of information, this would be much more useful if it was placed on a map, showing the exact location of the item. I started making the product on a map, printed the map on my laser printer, then laminating it in plastic to preserve it. Soon, I started branching out and made many such maps for all over the United States. I would go to trade shows in different States and sell my maps. Soon, at one trade show, a book publisher saw my product, and asked me if I would be interested in doing a book to show this information for the entire USA. I agreed, and I earned tens of thousands of dollars from this simple idea that I could easily knock out on the computer.

Another instance of this idea put to use was done by a friend of mine. My friend did some work for a hospital. One time, he stopped by the office of the hospital administrator and he noticed that some employees were busy making address labels – by hand. He asked about this, and they told him that anytime the hospital wanted to do a mailing, they had to hand print all of the labels for mailing. He asked why they didn't do it on the computer, and they said that they didn't know how. Well, my friend made a proposal to the hospital administration, and they hired him to do the label printing by computer. He quite easily imported the data into his computer, set up a database of all the people on the mailing list, and set it up to be printed on mailing labels. The whole job took only a few hours, and once it was done, and saved, the database could be used every time that labels were needed. For this, the hospital paid him thousands of dollars – every time that labels were needed! He did the work once, and got paid dozens of times for the job. He actually ended up netting well into the 6 figures by simply printing address labels.

Watch for any kind of opportunities like this where you can take advantage of inefficiencies in the marketplace! While places like hospitals and such are fully computerized now in the States, here in the Philippines you can still find such inefficiencies. You can make money from this.

# 34 – BALIKBAYAN BOX SERVICE

This chapter is really keyed in for people who live in the Philippines, want to live in the Philippines or have an interest in the Philippines. It is such a good idea that I just had to include it in this book, though, even if I decided to go more international on this edition of this book. Truth is, even if you have no interest in the Philippines, you could still do this, but it is of more interest to people who know and understand the Philippines.

This is an idea that I have had for a decade or so now, and I really believe that it can make a nice amount of money. It might take a few years to build up a big enough customer base to be real profitable, but in the out years, this could turn into a cash cow, in my opinion.

My idea is a Balikbayan Box forwarding service. As you might know, a Balikbayan box is a big box (usually 24" x 24" x 18") that can be shipped from the USA (or other Western countries) to the Philippines. The weight of the box does not affect the shipping price, that is only determined by the size of the box. For the typical large Balikbayan Box of the size that I mentioned, you will pay $60 to $120 to ship it from the USA, depending on the location where it is shipped from. For the cheapest shipping, try to locate your business on the West Coast of the USA, preferably around LA or San Francisco.

Now, in order to do this business, you will need to base your operations in the USA (or whatever country you wish to serve). You must have a location in a place where people wish to ship items to the Philippines.

Why is there a demand to ship things from the USA to the Philippines? Well, because the consumer market is limited in the Philippines in many ways. So many Filipinos have lived and worked overseas at some time in their lives that they have come to like products from abroad, but they can't get those products in the Philippines. Also, imported products can be very expensive in the Philippines, sometimes up to 3 or 4 times the price that you would pay in the USA. So, shipping items in a box from the USA to the Philippines can be a big cost saver compared to buying those products here in the Philippines.

**Here is how the idea will work:**

As you can imagine, almost every expat (and many Filipinos) who live in a different country always wants stuff from "back home." For an example, and American who lives in the Philippines might have certain foods that he misses, or office supplies that are cheaper in the States, or just about anything that he likes, but can't get a hold of here.

The idea is that you can set up a service, similar to a mail forwarding service, where you will forward balikbayan boxes. For example, you will give each customer an address where they can have packages shipped to. It is the address of your business, and a "suite" number, which is just an arbitrary number that will be assigned individually to each client.

So, a customer can go online and order goods, have them shipped to your address, and you will toss his shipment into his Balikbayan Box whenever it arrives. When the Box is full, you simply ship it to your client in the Philippines.

In addition to accepting deliveries for your clients, you can also add a shopping service, where one of your employees could go purchase the items that the client wants for his Balikbayan Box shipment. Of course, you can charge a markup on the price of the products that you go purchase for the client.

To make money on this service, you would simply charge a price for doing the work for the client. You can also charge an annual fee for the service in addition to the per box charges.

I am certain that this is a viable idea, because I have surveyed other expats here in the Philippines, and they all want to use such a service. I would like to offer it myself, but I have been unable to find the right person in the States to be my partner.

# 35 – FILL YOUR OWN NEEDS

If you are an expat, living in a different country than where you were born and lived most of your life, you surely find items that you miss from back home.

Every time that you want or need something and it is not easy to get or achieve, that is a business opportunity! Start pushing yourself to think this way, watch for ideas to come along, and soon you'll hit on something that can make you money.

When you live in a foreign country like the Philippines, you will always find that there are things you miss from back home. Often times it is a type of food that is not available in your new Country. For instance, I love black licorice, yet it is virtually impossible to find here in the Philippines (at least in my area), because local people either don't like it or are unfamiliar with it, meaning that there is no demand. Thus, no stores have black licorice.

Watch yourself, and listen to your thoughts. Every time that you say to yourself, "I wish I could get x" that is an opportunity to make money. You see, if you want that certain item, you can bet that there are thousands of other expats in the country who would also like to get that as well.

Now, the key on something like this is that it is not easy! I mean, it's not available in stores, so it's not easy to get, right? Well, figure out a way to get it, and then supply it to yourself and also to other expats who miss it and want it! You can make a huge mark-up on something that people want and miss, and are also unable to get!

This idea extends well beyond food items too. For example, maybe there is a service that you enjoyed using back home, but is unavailable here in the Philippines or wherever you live. Or, maybe the service is available, but done in a much different way that you don't like, or are uncomfortable with. Start up a business offering that service in the style that you are comfortable with, and other expats or Filipinos who have lived overseas might just beat a path to your door.

You know, here in the Philippines, as in any country, they do things differently than they do in other countries. No matter where you live you may find this to be true there too. No two countries are identical to each other. That doesn't mean that the way they do things in one country is right and the other is wrong, it only means that the two methods are different. Well, as we get older, we really become creatures of habit, and we like things to be done in the way that we are accustomed to. Take advantage of that desire by offering such services done in the way it was done back home, offer to do it the "right" way for other expats who live in the area, and you will likely garner some customers for your service!

# 36 – PRIVATE INVESTIGATION SERVICE

I get e-mails all the time from people who want or need some kind of investigation to be done here in the Philippines. Since these people who e-mail me are generally overseas (not in the Philippines), it is virtually impossible (or very expensive) for them to check into the situation themselves. They need somebody like me, or you, to do the checking. Such services can be provided no matter where you live.

One note of caution, before you move ahead with this arrangement, you should check out the laws of your locale. In many places, private investigators must be licensed by the government. Even if this is the case and you are not licensed, that is OK, there is a way that you can arrange things so that you can still do this service and also remain within the law.

How can you remain within the law if you are not licensed? To be honest, it is quite easy. Many people who are licensed investigators are not web savvy. They do not have a website, or really any way of advertising internationally. How do I know? Because I have been operating an Investigative service for many years already, so I follow this sort of stuff. The way you can do this, and keep things legal is that you will advertise on the web, and when somebody inquires, you make a deal with them. You then hire a local licensed private investigator to handle the work. You charge a price that is higher than the local investigator will charge you, you pay the investigator his price and the rest is your commission for arranging the deal. Everything is legal, you are getting the work done that the client needs, and you are inserting money into the local economy!

Most of the people who request such help from me are western men who have chat-mates, pen pals or other relationships with Filipinas. Maybe they are thinking of getting married to this girl that they know only through the Internet. Well, a lot of times, these guys are worried that the woman may not be genuine, and they want to find out before making the long trip to see them.

When I get such requests, I am happy to help, but I don't do it for free. Sometimes these guys get angry at me and tell me that I should not charge to do a few checks for them. But, if I did it for free, I could literally spend my entire day, every day of the week, every week of the year doing this, and since it would all be for free, how would my family eat dinner?

That said, I generally charge $150 to $200 per day for such a service. I usually farm the work out to one of my relatives (usually my brother-in-law) and I pay him a percentage of what I am being paid. I usually base my fee on how many days I think that the investigation will take, and tell the client that if the investigation takes longer than I expect, there will be an additional charge.

In a case like this one, where a guy wants to find out if his online girlfriend is genuine, my brother-in-law will usually just go the city where the girl lives, find her, and watch her. Maybe she has a lot of boyfriends who are hanging out with her? Maybe she is married? Maybe she really is genuine. He can find these answers by observing her for a day or two in most cases. After he completes his part of the investigation, he informs me of his findings, I write up a report for the client, and I e-mail it to him. Sometimes we have photos to include, or other items.

There are other things that people want investigated too, and we do those as well. I have investigated things like Philippine companies that have ripped off foreign investors. I have searched for people who are foreigners living in the Philippines, and their family "back home" wants to track them down. There are lots of different things that you may be asked to look into.

An area where you would likely get a lot of business too, is in searching for foreigners living in the Philippines, or whatever country you reside in, who are "wanted" in their home countries. For instance, there are literally hundreds (perhaps thousands) of expats living here who are wanted for child support evasion, crimes back home, etc. This could turn into a very lucrative market for you.

I have gotten quite a few such Investigative jobs, and I haven't even advertised to do such jobs. If you set up a true service and put up a website for this, I have no doubt that you can do a nice piece of business in this field.

# 37 – PROMOTE REAL ESTATE

As I suggested in another chapter of this book, no matter where you live on this earth, if you start up a website about your area and become a recognized expert about the place where you live, it will open up a lot of money making opportunities for you.

Becoming an expert can earn you money in a number of different ways. The way that I want to discuss in this chapter is that when you are an expert you can then start helping people who want to move to your area to find houses or land where they can build a house. For houses, this would include rental properties or property for sale. You can make a nice bit of money this way, and with relatively little work.

Last year, I had one website that I was planning to shut down, simply because it didn't make much money. While I loved the site a lot, and spent a lot of time on this particular site, the financial rewards from this site were quite small. So small, in fact, that it just wasn't worth my time any longer. I was right on the edge of just shutting it down when a friend advised me that I should "think outside the box" and come up with other ways of making money from the site. All of the ingredients were already in place. The site had a ton of visitors and traffic. I was using Google AdSense on the site, but it simply didn't pay me much money.

One of the reasons why I feel that this site did not perform well with Google AdSense is because it is a very "community" related site. The visitors come back day in and day out, and they simply became blind to the ads that were there. So, following my friend's advice, I started looking for other ways of monetizing the site.

One of the ways that I stumbled upon was selling real estate. My wife and I had recently purchased some land on a resort island, a really beautiful place. Every time that I wrote about the place on my website, I would get lots of questions about it. There was certainly interest in the place.

I decided to put up an ad for property on the Island. My wife had connections with several land owners on the Island who were willing to pay her referral commissions for each purchase made. You know what, it worked great! The first day that I advertised the real estate service, my wife got 10 e-mails inquiring about purchasing land there too. And, it didn't slow down.

This turned into a very well paying pursuit for my wife. She sold so many lots that she ended up turning that website into my number 1 money maker for an informational site. She turned a very nice profit.

And, why not? I mean, Feyma knows a lot about the property there, since we own there ourselves. She has connections to the right people on the island who have property to sell. Through my website, I have connections to people who are interested in purchasing land. It was a match made in heaven! Again, if you become an expert in your area, and you have a website which you can use to promote the area, there is no reason why you cannot follow the pattern that we took.

So, as you can see, you can also set yourself up for a great money making idea like this as well. It has worked super for me, and you can easily duplicate this in the area where you choose to call home!

# 38 – PUT YOUR EXPERIENCE TO WORK

Do you have some kind of expertise that is in demand? If so, put it to work! Let me give you the story of somebody that I know who moved to the Philippines in the last year or so.

This fellow had years of experience in AutoCAD design. AutoCAD work is something that is in demand worldwide. He always told me that he really needed to find a job here in the Philippines, because he needed the income to sustain his life here. I advised him that finding a regular job was not the way to go. Rather, he should try to get into outsourcing. I recommended that he should do two things. First, find US companies who needed AutoCAD design done, and would be willing to hire my acquaintance to get the job done for them. Next, he should find maybe a half dozen Filipino AutoCAD designers who were looking for work here. Next, he could take on jobs from these US companies (or from anywhere in the world), let the Filipino designers do the work, then this fellow could simply review each job to make sure that it was done properly, and that no errors had been made.

Under this system, he could put the power of inexpensive labor in the Philippines to his advantage, while taking on jobs from developed countries, and make a very nice profit. Unfortunately, this fellow did not decide to follow this path, but it is a viable way to earn money, I have no doubt about that.

How can you find people to pay you for doing these kinds of jobs? It's quite easy, actually. There are plenty of websites where companies can put up a listing for a job that they need to have done, and then people like you and I can put in bids to do the work. This is really a perfect way to leverage your living in the Philippines, it gives you an opportunity to lead the life you want, in the place where you want to live, while also giving jobs to some Filipinos, and earning money for yourself. In my opinion, putting together something like this is really a great solution! No matter what your expertise, if it is in demand anywhere in the world, I have no doubt that you can put a system like this to work, and profit from it. The key, in my mind is to not do the work yourself, there is only so much that a single person can do. However, since you have the expertise, you can put local people to work, and you review their work, supervise, and also be the person to get jobs from foreign companies!

# 39 – TRANSLATION WORK

I have several friends who do translation work, and make good money doing it. Basically, you would need to set up a website to advertise your services, and then offer yourself as a translator. Lots of businesses all around the world will have documents that they need to have translated. Individuals will pay for this too. So, basically, if you can speak multiple languages, you can do translation. Brush up on the languages that you know, and you can translate any language you know into any other language you know. This can be hired out, and people will pay a good price for the service too. This is especially true if you know uncommon languages, and somebody needs translation into (or from) that language. The more rare a language is, the higher the price you can charge for the translation, because there will be few others who are providing services for that language.

Another thing that you might consider is that you could hire a staff of people who speak each speak a different language. Let's say that you get a request for a translation of a document from Russian to Chinese – you have one person translate it, and another of your staff read it over to see if it really makes sense in Chinese. This way, you are using your various people with different skills not only to translate but also to do Quality Assurance work by checking the work of their peers.

So, if you know multiple languages (or can hire a staff who does), this might be the perfect business for you. It is very inexpensive to get into this business, all you need is a computer, e-mail, and you are ready to get started!

# 40 – TOUR SERVICES

Here we go again. Remember how I was talking earlier about having a website about the area where you live? I said that you need to make yourself the "go-to guy" for the area. Well, if you can establish yourself on the web as an important contact for the area, you can continue to add other services that you can offer and make money from.

How about Airport pickups? Most people who are traveling to your town for the first time would love to have contact with a local resident, and get some "scoop" on the area. You can offer a paid pickup service at the airport. Once picking up the person, you can take them for a quick drive around town, showing them the important things and places that they might want or need to find out about for a successful visit to your area!

How about offering tours of the area? Maybe there is a landmark or something of importance in your area, you can offer a paid tour to the place. Frankly, there are so many ideas that you can employ in the field of offering services to tourists! It can be a very lucrative market for you!

# 41 – TURN A HOBBY INTO A BUSINESS

This might sound a little "fairy-tale-ish" to some who are reading this, but honestly, you can turn a hobby into a successful business. For example, if you enjoy photography, you could become a freelance photographer. I particular like the freelance photography idea, because I also enjoy taking photos.

There are several ways that you can turn photography into a money making endeavor.

First, be vigilant in keeping a camera with you at all times, and take a lot of photos. You never know when some newsworthy event will happen, and if you are on the scene with a camera, you may be able to sell the photos to newspapers or news agencies. I have had this happen to me twice since living in the Philippines. The first time was when I lived in General Santos City. On New Year Day, 2002, we experienced a large earthquake in General Santos, measuring 7.2 on the Richter scale. As an avid photographer, I went out into town almost immediately after the quake (around 5am) and started shooting photos. Electricity was out all over town, but it happened that I owned the only Internet Cafe in town that had a generator to keep the place online even during brown-outs. Because of this, I was able to get a lot of good earthquake photos, and also was the only person who was able to transmit these photos to the major newspapers and news agencies. I sold a lot of photos that day, and made a fair amount of money from doing nothing but taking photos. The next day, every major Daily Newspaper in Manila featured photos that I took on the front page of their publications. It's a good feeling to go to the news-stand and see your pictures on every newspaper that they are offering for sale!

In another incident, in April 2002, there was a bombing that occurred in General Santos, just 30 meters or so outside one of our businesses there. I immediately grabbed my camera and started shooting photos. Again, I had major newspapers and also news agencies like Reuters and AP buying my photos. If I went to major websites like CNN.com and Yahoo, my photos of the bombing were plastered on their front pages! It is quite a feeling to go to Yahoo.com and see a photo that you took right on their front page! I made a good amount of money in both of these incidents, and you can do this sort of thing too.

OK, we both know that these kind of news events don't happen every day, and even when they do happen it is kind of the luck of the draw to be on the scene and also to have a camera with you. There is another way to profit from photography, though. You see, there are a lot of Stock Photography sites coming online now where you can sell your photos! You, as a photographer, can put up a gallery of your photos, and people will buy them. You and the stock photo site will share in the money. I have been both a photo buyer and a seller on these sites over the years. My favorite site for this is Dreamstime.com.

So, if you have other hobbies, think about it and figure out how you can make money from the hobby. It will both give you something to do in order to keep busy, and also a little extra income! Maybe you could set up a website about your hobby and profit from advertising placed on your site. Maybe you can set up courses where you teach others about the endeavor. One thing I am sure of, no matter the hobby, there is a way to earn from it. You just have to analyze it and figure out how.

# 42 – CONFERENCE CALL

A lot of my ideas in this book are like building blocks. If you do one of the ideas, another of the ideas then becomes possible. When you do that second idea, a third idea can then come into play. This one fits that category.

If you have done many of the ideas to build up your credibility, to build up your popularity, and to establish yourself as an expert on the topic that you write about, then this idea might be the next logical step.

Once a month, or even more frequently (or less), do a conference call where people will pay to be included. Another popular option would be a webinar, which has become quite popular these days.

For example, I consider myself an expert on the subject of an expat living in the Philippines. I have written about the subject for a long time, and there are a lot people who would also recognize that I am an expert on the subject. Because of this expertise, a lot of people will pay to talk with me on the telephone, ask me questions, and get my insight on the topic.

For a service like this, you can actually charge people for your time. You can actually do one-on-one calls, but if you have enough requests, it is better to do a conference call. The reason I feel that  conference call is better in my opinion is that people will get added value by hearing the questions from other people and your answers to them. For example, "Steve" might have had a question in mind to ask you, but as he listens in, he might hear a half dozen questions and answers that prove valuable to him. I do recommend having a fixed limit to the number of people who are allowed on each call. This does two things – it makes for more "exclusivity" and thus, makes the call seem more valuable to the listener. Secondly, it makes each person be able to have a chance to ask their question, and receive an answer. For example, if you had 200 people participating on a one hour conference call, it would not be possible for each of them to have time for a personal question.

The more popular you become, the more valuable your opinion is considered, the better this particular idea will work. Don't do it as a first business, because you won't have customers. But, as you have taken time and built up your reputation, you will find that this kind of thing will open up to you, and you can make money offering advice like this.

If you decide to offer a "one-on-one" call service, you can charge a higher price for that, because of the exclusivity of the thing. I mean, the customer has you exclusively, without interruption. Charge a premium price for this, and also, set a time limit on how long the call can last, or surcharge if the call goes longer.

As I said earlier, you could consider a conference call or a webinar. Another similar option would be something that Google offers called a "Hangout on the Air". This is much like a webinar, and it can accommodate up to 100 people. It is a sort of video conference call. Another cool thing about a Hangout on the Air is that these Hangouts on the Air are automatically recorded and put on your YouTube Channel. You could then let people access the Hangouts for free, or you could charge for access to the Hangout videos on your own website, and source of potential revenue in your pocket!

Don't underprice your expertise.

# 43 – FLIP PROPERTIES

If you just get in your car and drive around here in the Philippines, you will find that there are signs hanging on trees, on signposts or just about anywhere here that say "House for Assume" - in other words, they are offering a house for sale, and all you have to do is pick up the payments. In some cases, they will want you to perhaps put up a small down payment to purchase their equity, but not always, sometimes they are simply willing to walk away from the property to get out from under the mortgage.

Certainly, while using different terminology, there are similar types of signs in locations all over the world.

Another way to find distressed properties is to simply go to banks and look for the foreclosed properties that they are offering. Generally, banks here in the Philippines will have a public bulletin board in their lobby with a list of photos and information about houses that they have foreclosed on, and are offering for quick sale. The terms on such properties are variable, and can be negotiated with the bank.

For me, I would prefer to deal directly with the property owner before the foreclosure happens, rather than with the bank. I feel that the property owner is more negotiable that way, but either way, you can pick up some nice deals on properties this way.

Many times, when you pick up a distressed property like this, the property is not in good shape. The worse shape it is in, generally the better the deal that you can pick up. The reason that the properties are often in poor shape is that if the people figure that they are about to be foreclosed upon, they often simply stop taking care of the place. The pride of ownership is gone, and thus, they neglect the property.

So, if you pick up such distressed property, you should figure that you will need to do some work on it to bring it back to the condition that you would want it to be in. Generally, you can hire very cheap labor here to take care of much of the physical work, you just need to stick around and supervise to make sure that it is done properly.

Once the place has been restored to acceptable condition you have two choices: Rent it out or Sell it! At this point, you need to look at the market and make a decision on which method will make the most money for you. If you sell the house then you can roll that money into buying another house immediately. If you rent the house, you can save up your rental income and eventually use it to purchase another property, although it would not happen immediately. Either way you will make money, just analyze it and decide which method is going to produce the best income potential for you over the longer term.

# 44 – BUILD AN APARTMENT COMPLEX

This chapter was written concerning the housing market in the Philippines where I reside. However, what is written here can apply to markets in developing countries all around the world! If you are in a developed country like the USA, Australia or many European countries, this chapter may not pan out for you.

I have talked a number of times about strategies about how I make money in the Philippines. To this point, I almost exclusively make my money through e-Commerce and advertising on my various websites. Any kind of investment adviser or financial planner will tell you one things when they advise you on how to build your wealth - DIVERSIFY. Put your money into a number of different venues and it will be safer for you. Let's say that you decide to put your money into the stock market, and you put it all into one company. If you do that, you could be in for trouble. If that one company runs into trouble, your money could go down the tube. If you spread it around to a lot of companies that is safer. If you put some money spread out in the stock market, put some into real estate, put some into other investments - that is true diversification, and in doing so you are offering your money a chance to grow and be safe at the same time.

At this time, I have my money and my efforts tied up into the internet. It is diversified to a point in that it is spread out into different activities and subject areas on the net, but it is still on on the net. I realize that I need to venture into other areas to make additional investments for my own protection, and also to take advantage of growth areas that I am currently ignoring. With that in mind, lately I have been doing some thinking about what I would want to do with my money to help me achieve my long term goals and enable myself to be comfortable as I get older.

Let me sidetrack for a moment, if you don't mind. About five years ago, I moved to a new home in Davao. I am in a different part of town from where I used to live. When you move to a new location, you tend to shop around and see what kind of houses or apartments are available on the market. My wife and I did quite a bit of shopping around for a place to live. One thing we noticed was that rental property goes quickly. If you see something that you like, you better snap it up, because if you wait even a few days it may be gone already. We found this particularly true of apartments, and especially for upscale apartments. Our family is too large for an apartment, so we rent a house. We did look at apartments, though, because a friend was moving at the same time and wanted one. We figured that we might as well include apartments in our search, just to know what was available. Every time that we found a nice apartment, it was either already rented, or rented quickly after we looked at it.

So, going back to my search for the right investment vehicle, and combining that with my observation about apartments, it seemed to me that building a small apartment building might be a good strategy for me. One saying that I've heard often about real estate is this - "they aren't making any more of it!" It's true. Real estate can go up or down in price, but the trend is always up over time. Keep in mind too, if you are a foreigner you cannot own land here. In my case, I am in a long term stable marriage to my Filipina wife. We've been married nearly 18 years now. I have no fears of the marriage breaking up, even in the long run. Because of this, I have no qualms about buying the property in my wife's name.

In my case, here in Davao City, there are number of foreigners. My target would be to rent the apartment units to foreigners. When renting to foreigners, you need to provide a more premium place, not just something that is built to the minimum standards. However, the rent will be higher. Generally speaking, a foreigner will probably take better care of the place as well. With the better building standards and the better care given to the unit, it will also mean that your investment will last longer. The units that I have in mind would be maybe 5 or 6 apartment units in the building. Let's say 6 units. I would rent 5 of the apartments on a long term lease for around P20,000 per month (minimum one year lease). The sixth unit, I would reserve for short term rentals to foreigners visiting Davao. I get lots of e-mails from people planning to vacation here and want somewhere to stay other than a hotel. I would rent this last unit for P13,000 or P15,000 per week.

An apartment building like what I have in mind would probably cost around P7M for the land and construction costs. That is equivalent to about $166,000. Let's say it costs $175,000. If I have full occupancy on the rentals, my monthly income would be:

Five units at P20,000 = P100,000

One unit at P13,000 per week = P13,000 x 4 weeks per month ⁻ P52,000

Total income for the month P100,000 + P52,000 = P152,000

Of course there will be expenses involved too. It is also possible that the unit for weekly rent may not be occupied all the time. Let's just say that my monthly take from the building after paying expenses is P120,000. That is enough income for a family of 4 people to live on easily.

My personal goal is to build four such apartment buildings. Four units, with each earning me around $3,000 per month, and I have an income of $12,000 per month. Why did I choose four units? I have four kids. When my wife and I pass, it would be my plan to leave one building for each of my kids. I have one child who is mentally challenged, and I doubt that he will ever be able to hold down a job that will make the kind of income that he will be needing. Something like an apartment building would make perfect sense in providing an income to sustain him.

In the United States, I had friends who were into these kind of real estate investments, and did well. I had never thought of something like this in the Philippines. Given my experience in searching for rental property, though, I believe that this is a good strategy.

# 45 – DO WHAT YOU ARE PASSIONATE ABOUT

Over my years of living in the Philippines, as you have read, I have done a lot of different things to make money here. I have failed, and I have succeeded. In the past 14 years or so, I have succeeded, almost exclusively. Because of my success in earning a living in the Philippines, the word has gotten out, and a lot of people think of me when they want to find out how to succeed here. I have never really promoted myself in this way, I have just done what I needed to do in order to live here, and it has worked. Because the word has spread about my ability to earn a living here, I get a lot of e-mails from people asking me basically the same question:

I want to live in the Philippines. How can I earn a living?

Well, because I get hundreds of such e-mails, this is a big reason why I decided to write this book. As part of this book, I want to tell you the answer I have given to nearly every e-mail asking the question above.

Follow your passion. If you do what you are passionate about, the money will follow.

I honestly believe that. Let me tell you, and I hope that this doesn't disappoint you... if you bought this book and you plan to just choose one of the 49 ideas I have listed here, and just do it, unless it is something that you are passionate about, you will probably fail. I am sorry, my friend, but this is just the truth. The number one consideration for you to make, in my opinion is to choose something that you love! Figure out what you are passionate about, and do it. Maybe at first you won't know how to earn money from it. That's OK, but do it anyway. Sooner or later (hopefully sooner) you will figure out ways to make money doing what you love doing. When you figure out how to earn money doing the thing that you love, you are set for a good and rewarding life!

For example, let's say that you love fishing. Well, the Philippines is an island nation, so the opportunities for fishing are nearly everywhere you look. That said, there is not much sport fishing available here. Let's say that you come to live here, and bring a full supply of fishing tackle, and such. You start fishing just for fun, and you really enjoy it. How can that make money?

Well, let's jot down a few ways that this hobby could be beneficial to you, financially:

For starters, you can eat the fish that you catch, thus saving money on groceries.

You can put up a website about fishing in the Philippines. Share your experiences. Include lots of photos of your fishing adventures. Write about the wonderful times that you have fishing in the Philippines. You'll be surprised, soon you'll gain visitors, and you can make money from advertising on your website.

As your website becomes more popular, you will start getting e-mails from people who are coming to the Philippines and want to fish. They will ask your advice on fishing in the Philippines. Start up a guide service, and charge these people to take them to places that you have been successful in your fishing. Becoming a guide and getting paid for fishing should be a dream occupation for somebody who loves to fish!

Write books about fishing in the Philippines. Maybe you'll write one book about what locations are good fishing areas. Another book could be about what kinds of fishing equipment are needed or useful in the Philippines. Perhaps another book could be a Photo book of your catches. You can write a number of books and self-publish them, selling them through your website.

If your guide business grows too large, teach some local people your fishing techniques, then hire them to take out fishermen every day. You might have 4 or 5 different fishing parties out each day, and thus really be multiplying your potential earnings.

These examples are only the tip of the iceberg. But, they are meant to show you that you can take a hobby, something that you are very passionate about, and you can use that passion to earn money.

If you choose to do something that you really don't care much about, you are likely to fail!

A lot of people e-mail me and ask me:

"What business can I start that will earn the most money there?"

I am sorry, but this is the wrong way to look at it. If the business that is generally the most profitable here is something that you absolutely hate doing, you are sure to fail, because you simply cannot maintain the interest required to make it successful. On top of that, if you hate doing it, that will come across to your customers, and they will simply go to somebody else to do their business, somebody who loves what they do. That is just nature. We all have different interests, and I guarantee that you will succeed the most when you do something that you enjoy and have a passion for!

# 46 – THINK OUTSIDE THE BOX

I constantly advise people to "Think outside the box!" What does that mean? Well, it means to think in different ways that are not the conventional way to think! Look at things from a different angle than the other 99% of people observe from. When you think outside the box, you will come up with a lot of ideas that will make good money!

Why? Because thinking outside the box will present unique opportunities to you that others are not doing. If there are already 40 places in town serving hamburgers, opening the 41st such place is not likely to make you rich. However, if you find a different twist on a burger that makes your burger fresh and interesting, you may have the 41st burger joint, but the difference is that your burger is unique! Some people won't care for it, because it is different. However, if only 10% of the people think that your unique burger is delicious, that is a huge slice of the market!

I mean, think about this. If you go into the burger business against 40 other places, and you are all selling basically the exact same thing, maybe you'll get 2% or so of the market. Much of your success (or lack of it) will be based on your location. If all 41 burger places have burgers that are the same, the customer will just go to the most convenient one, closest to his house or office, right? But, if your burger is different in some way, and this particular customer loves your unique taste, he might drive past 4 or 5 other places to get to your place! He might even drive clear across town, because he loves your burger so much.

There are lots of different kinds of businesses, and we don't live on burgers alone, no doubt on that, but you can apply this strategy to any kind of business.

A while back, I was driving through Davao, the city in which I live, and I saw a new business that had recently opened for business. It was a combination of a Meat Store, Hair Dresser and an Internet Cafe. Now, that guy was really thinking outside the box! I have to say, that I personally don't see the connection between these three, this guy might have thought of something that I am not aware of. It is crazy ideas like this that will often surprise you and be wildly successful!

Don't be afraid to be different! You never know when you will hit upon a success.

# SECTION 7 - BOOKS

Books are a key money making strategy.

# 47 – WRITE EBOOKS

I honestly believe that every one of us is an expert on something. It might be Nuclear Engineering or maybe it's Basket Weaving, but we all know at least one subject so well that we could be considered an expert. If your expertise is something like Basket Weaving, there is nothing wrong with that! Some of us think that the thing that we know well is not important enough to consider ourselves an "expert" or for that to mean something important. That kind of thinking, though, is wrong! The very fact that we have expertise on any subject makes the information valuable, and you can make money with that information!

Why not write some how-to books? Whether you are an expert on a complex subject or a simple one, you can bet that there are people who are willing to pay for your expertise, because they want to do that thing that you know so well too!

Writing a book does not mean that you need to have a publisher either. You can be your own publisher! For example, this very book that you are reading right now is self-published! And, even if I only sell 1 copy for every 10 that a "big publisher" could sell, I will likely still make more money from this effort than if I had gone with a big publisher! Did you know that people who have books published by big publishing companies rarely make very much money on the effort?

If you self-publish, there are two ways that you can go, too. You can make your book an e-book (electronic book) that will just simply be downloaded from the Internet. Or, you can use a POD company (Print On Demand) where they simply print a book for the customer on a one by one basis, as they are sold. For this, you can check with companies like CreatSpace, a POD company which is owned by Amazon.

And, you don't need to just write one book. Keep writing more and more, and keep offering all of your titles. Maybe in two years you can put 5 or 6 books together. I advocate selling your books for a minimum of $29.99 each. So, let's say that you sell 200 copies of each book per year at $29.99. That means that you would bring in almost $36,000 per year if you have 6 books to sell. Maybe you won't do that well, but maybe you'll do better too!

I have one eBook that I have had on the market for about 8 years now. I sell that title for $49, and have sold about 4,000 copies in 8 years (about 500 copies per year). That is nearly $200,000 in income over the life of the book so far. Not bad, huh? With all of my books together, I earn a monthly income of about $2,000 or more per month, every month. So, you can put together some decent money from writing your own books and self-publishing them. On top of that, my books are at least 95% self-sold as well, selling solely through my website.

How will you market the book? Well, mainly through your own website! If you have a website that you have built up to the point where it is even marginally popular, you have a built in audience of people who have an interest to buy your book! After all, you have shown that you are an expert on the subject that you are writing about!

Another marketing technique you can use to target titles that will sell is to put up pages to announce titles that you have not even written yet. Say that it is "in production" at this time, and people can sign up to be notified when the book is ready. If you get no inquiries, or even just a very few, you can cancel your plans to write that title and move on to something that will be more in demand. As an added way of checking the demand, you could even start an advertising campaign with Google AdWords or some other Pay per Click Ad company, advertise the book on related sites, and see what happens with demand.

Think about it, start writing, and then start seeing the money roll in. You can do it!

## How to publish and sell an e-book

First, let's start with the most basic question that some of you are asking right now... what is an "e-book"? Well, an e-book is an electronic book. Basically, when you write a book, it is usually printed on paper, and bound. A reader can take a book along with him when he goes somewhere, carrying it in his hand or in a backpack or some other suitable carrying method. Alternatively, an e-book or electronic book is when you write a book and publish it digitally. Instead of being printed on paper, it is a computer file, usually a PDF file that can be stored on a computer, on a flash drive, CD or any other method of storing a digital file. To read an e-Book, a reader can do it on a computer, on his cellular phone, on an e-Book reader like pictured above, or through other methods that can display a digital file.

Why would anybody publish an e-book? There are a number of factors. One of the most important is cost. If you want to publish a paper book, that costs money. You write the book, probably on a computer with some kind of word processing software. After the book is done, you format it with some kind of publishing software, and you send it either to a publisher, or a printer. If you have a publishing company who is going to publish the book for you,

you will send them the electronic files and they will take care of the printing and the distribution of the paper book. If you want to self-publish a paper book, you can do that too. You will hire a printer to print up the books, bind them and ship them to you. This will cost you a fair amount of money to have done.

One of the big downsides of a regular paper book is that usually you will need to have a fair number of the books printed and bound, in order to take advantage of getting the work done in bulk. You usually cannot print up just 3 or 4 books just to see "how it sells". If you are a well-established writer and have a track record of selling a lot of books, getting 10,000 or even 100,000 books printed up is not a big deal, you have a basis to believe that selling that many copies will not be a problem, based on previous results. However, if you are a relatively new writer, or if you are writing on a very niche topic, it might be hard to sell even 1,000 copies of your book. Is it worth it to write a book if you are not going to be able to sell even 1,000 copies? It sure can be, we'll get into that a bit later in this guide.

So, given that it is expensive to print and publish a regular book, why not just get a publisher to do it? After all, they will pay for all of the printing and binding costs. They will also take care of distribution of the book. Basically, after you write the book, they will take care of everything, all you have to do is cash the checks and spend the money. But, wait. How much money will you make? The truth is that you will be doing pretty good if you can get paid 10% of the cover price of the book. So, if the book is $20, you will be doing good to get $2 as your royalty. In fact, you may only get $1 or $1.50 per book sold. Another catch is that there will be lots of things subtracted from your royalties too, bringing your effective payment per book down to as low as only half of what has been promised to you. In fact, if you get $1 per book after all of the deductions, you will be doing pretty good.

Well, your first problem in finding a publisher is that if you are a new writer it can be very hard to find somebody who is willing to take a chance on your unproven skills. Most publishers will have no interest in signing you on, unless you have a track record of selling books previously. That's kind of a catch 22 situation because you can't sell any books until somebody has already published for you, and you can't get published unless you have a track record of selling books! What can you do?

Enter the e-book. With the e-book you can write the book, publish it and sell it all yourself! Now, the key there is that you need to have an audience that follows you so that there will be people to buy the book. You need to be an authority on the subject if you want people to spend their money to buy your book. How can you become an authority? How can you gain an audience that follows you? In these days of Internet communications, that is actually not very difficult. Get a website of your own and build a following of readers. Get active on social networking sites like Facebook or LinkedIn, or one of the many others. The more people who follow you, the bigger your potential book buying audience.

Now, when I say to get a website, what do I mean? I am not saying that you should start writing about any topic under the sun. You don't write today about buying a new car, then tomorrow about baking a cupcake recipe. If you skip around to lots of topics like that, it will be hard to build a following, and also it will be hard to convince anybody that you are enough of an expert on any topic that they will want to buy your book. However, you need to focus on a narrow topic and write about that. You need a niche.

**What is a niche?**

A niche is a narrow topic. As an example, the topic of Cooking is quite broad. There are so many things that you can cook. Maybe you narrow the topic down to Cooking Desserts. Want to go more narrow than that? How about Cooking Pastry? Getting even more narrow, we can go back to the topic that I mentioned earlier, how to cook cupcakes. Let's say you start a website all about how to cook cupcakes. You write about cupcake recipes. You write about frosting recipes. You write about why certain types of frosting are better to use for decorating the cupcakes. You write about cupcake decorating competitions. There are lots and lots of topics you can write about within this quite narrow "niche" topic.

So, you write a new article every day for a year or so, and pretty soon your website has 1,000 people who follow every day. Now it's time to write that book. So, you have decided to write a book called "How to start a successful cupcake business". You write the book and have it all complete with great instructions, great easy to read text, some nice pictures and such. Everything is ready to go. What do you do next?

Well, your first step is to decide how you are going to publish the book. You have never written a book in your life, so it is going to be very difficult to find a publisher for the book.

Let's say, though, that you do find a publisher. Because of your inexperience they will pay you a lower rate, though. Let's say that the book is $20, and you will be paid a royalty of $1.25 per copy. After other expenses (such as damaged books, returns on books that retailers didn't sell and such) let's say that you end up with 80 cents per book by the end of the deal. Let's just say that you sell 10,000 books by the end of the deal. So, by going the way of the publisher, you made $800 after everything was said and done. That's not a lot of money, probably doesn't even pay you minimum wage for the time you spent doing the writing and research.

Let's look at the e-book option. Let me tell you right up front that you will sell a lot fewer e-books than if your book is published on paper and available in bookstores. Still, though, let's look at the math.

You write the book and publish it as a PDF file, which people can purchase over the Internet and they can download it when they pay for it. It costs you nothing but your time to write and "publish" the e-book. You may pay a small amount of money to set up the website, let's say $100 for all of the website expenses (you can do it for far less than that, but we'll say $100). In addition, you will have some small amount of fees to pay for the money end of the transaction when somebody buys the e-book. Let's say that it costs you $1.30 per book that you sell, and $10 per month as a flat fee for the sales. I will explain later in the book how all of this works, and why you will be paying these fees, but for now, just accept that you will pay $10 per month and $1.30 per book sold). So, the book is $20, as it was in the "publisher" example. You keep the entire $20, less the fees I noted. So, let's say that in one year, you sell just 10% of the number of books that a publisher can sell. That would mean that in 1 year you will sell 1,000 books. Since the retail price of the book is $20, that is $20,000 in one year. However, you have to pay those fees. Your $10 per month fee will come to $120 for 1 year.

The per book fee of $1.30 for 1,000 books will come to $1,300. So, the total fees you will pay, $1,300 plus $120 will come to a total of $1,420. Your book sales came to a total of $20,000. Your final net profit comes to $18,580.

Hmm... you let somebody else publish and sell the book and your profit for selling 10,000 books comes to $800. You publish it yourself and sell it yourself, and only sell 1,000 books, but your profit is over $18,000? Not bad, huh? And, believe me, this is very possible. The whole key to this, though, is that you need to build up that following that I mentioned. You need to have a thousand or more people reading your website. You need to build up more followers on social network sites. When you do what it takes to build these "sales generators" up, this kind of profit is not only possible, it is likely.

Now, think about this.. I just showed you an example where you can make a realistic profit of over $18,000 in just one year. However, there is no reason why you can't have multiple e-book titles on the market! You don't have to limit yourself to just the one book about "How to set up a successful cupcake business," no, you can also publish other titles that play to your audience, maybe things like:

- 101 Cupcake Recipes

- 30 Frosting Recipes

- Decorating techniques of the pros

How about a monthly newsletter listing surplus commercial baking equipment for sale? You can charge for that too. To be honest, the possibilities are virtually endless.

Let's say that you get 5 different eBooks up for sale at various prices. Maybe you will earn $50,000 in the first year. Want to know another secret that will make you happy? When you go with a publisher, you will have a contract with a certain ending date. Maybe it is 1 or 2 years in length. After your contract is over, they will not print up any more of your books.

But, when you self-publish an e-book, you are in control. There is no cost in producing another copy. So, you can sell that e-book in perpetuity. Not only that, but there is also an opportunity for updated versions. In 2012, you can come out with the "2012 Updated Version of How to set up a successful cupcake business" with all the latest information from the expert in the field! That means that all of those people who bought the original publication are candidates for the newly updated version. Since you sold the book to them directly, you have their e-mail addresses, and can send out a "sales letter" e-mail to let them know that a new version is available. Let's say you have sold 3,000 copies of the book already, and you e-mail each of those previous buyers. Maybe you will sell 500 of the new update in the first month to previous happy buyers! That's a $10,000 quick profit in the first month that the new book is available.

So, as you can see, there are possibilities for lots of follow on sales, plenty of marketing that you can do yourself. The possibilities for money-making are really available for the picking.

So, if I have sold you on the idea, let's look at how to actually do it.

**The Mechanics of How to Do It!**

Choosing your topic

A lot of people ask me how to choose what to write about. I always tell them that they should write about something that they enjoy, something they have a passion for. In addition, they should write about something that they know about, or can learn about before they start writing.

A friend of mine recently told me that if a person wants to choose what they should write about, a good way to choose is by first studying various tools that are available that will help you determine what topics have the most demand. You can actually use some online tools to find out what people search for on the Internet. So, the logical thing to so would be to use one of those tools to find out what a lot of people are searching for, and start writing about that.

I do not believe in that. Some people, maybe even my friend, will think I am foolish for throwing away such valuable tools. However, I don't think it is a foolish thing to do. Why? Because no matter what you decide to write about, there are people all over

the world who have an interest similar to yours. Yes, your audience may be smaller, but there will still be enough of an audience who will buy your products, if you are truly an expert and have passion for the topic. Having passion about what you are writing about shows through to your readers, and it makes your writing compelling – people will want to read what you write and know what you are saying.

If you just use some online tool to search and find out what lots of people want to learn about, you will not have the passion that you would if you were writing on a topic that is near to your heart. I, personally, believe that passion is the most important thing when it comes to choosing your topic. I have never used a tool to help me decide what I should write about. I write what I enjoy, and even when others try to dictate what they want me to write about, unless they suggest something that is of serious interest to me, I thank them for the suggestion, but I don't write about the topic. Staying genuine with your readers and with yourself is more important than chasing dollars, and if you stick with something that you have passion for, the dollars will come, regardless of how small your niche is.

Another thing to consider when choosing a very small niche is that the fewer people are interested in the topic, that also means that there are fewer writing about it, so you have less competition to deal with as well. So, my sincere advice is to write about something that interests you.

Of course, your first step is that if you want to successfully market and sell your e-Book you need to build up an audience, a group of followers. A big part of this is that you need to develop expertise on a certain topic, and you need to share your expertise with people. How can you build an audience for even a small niche? Use tools like Facebook, Twitter and your own website to bring others who are interested in your niche into your audience!

Over time, you will grow a group of people who will follow you with great interest. Who is this group of people? You can make them into your own online community! These are all people who also have an interest in the same niche that you are interested in.

You want to make yourself an expert on that niche and lead this online community. When you do that, you have a great target audience of customers for your book!

This particular step is outside the subject area of this particular eBook, but if you don't know how to do this you can check some of our other publications. The ones you might find interesting on this topic would include:

- How to set up your own blog

- How to build a community online

It will take you time to build up an online community that is big enough to make your book writing successful, but if you put the effort into it, believe me, your time and effort will pay off nicely for you.

When you have reached "critical mass" and have a big enough audience of readers and followers, it's time to start thinking of starting to write some e-books and making some money from your knowledge.

Your next step is obvious... write the book! You can use any type of word processing software for this. I personally use Open Office, which a free Office Productivity software. Most people use Microsoft Products, and Microsoft Office, specifically Microsoft Word is the application where you will probably want to get started in writing.

Simply write a complete text on the topic that you are covering. All of the "how-to" and such. Format the book in the size and such that you choose, within your word processing program that you are using.

When writing, remember that things like spelling and grammar are important. These days, a lot of people tend to forget about things like spelling and grammar, especially younger people who are used to abbreviating everything when doing things like Instant Messaging or Texting. This is a mistake, because a large number of people, especially those with money to spend on your book, are older and not into the whole "texting" type of abbreviations. With a computer, it is very easy to use a spell checker, so do it! Be careful, though, a spell checking software cannot usually tell the difference between words like "to, too or two" so you have to make sure that you check those manually. Many people, me included, are turned off when they open a book and see a ton of misspelled words, and they instantly discount anything else that the author says, based on the fact that they don't even know how to spell. Now, having said that, nobody is perfect. If you search this very book, you may well find an error or two. If you make a few mistakes that go uncaught when you check the book, that is not a deal killer. However, if you write a book and every sentence contains multiple words that are misspelled, bad grammar and such, well, it will tend to undermine your credibility and result in few book sales in the future.

So, write the book using some sort of Word Processing software, whichever one suits you, then be sure to edit it. Spell Check the book. Better yet, have somebody else check it for mistakes in spelling and grammar, because we often overlook our own mistakes, and others will spot them more quickly. Make it clear to the person who does the checking that you will not be offended, rather you will be grateful if they point out your mistakes.

To keep your text more readable, spice it up a bit. Some text, if it is important should probably be typed in a bold font to give the words more emphasis. Maybe some things you type should be in italics. Why should you do these things? It breaks up the monotony of the text and makes it easier to read.

Another thing that you should make sure you include is some pictures and other such graphics. The reason for this are twofold. Firstly, it serves the same purpose I made in the previous paragraph, it breaks things up and keeps the book more readable. Second reason is that an image might be able to drive your point home.

Remember the old saying, "a picture is worth a thousand words"? Well, it really can be true!

Remember, you want to make your book easy for your reader to read and digest. Why? Because you want your reader to enjoy reading the book, and come away informed. If he feels like that, he may go buy another of your books! If he finds the book difficult to read, he may never finish it, and will certainly not be buying any more of your books!

Next, you want to export, or save your document as a PDF file. PDF is a format developed by Adobe a number of years ago. PDF, also called "Acrobat" is a format that can be viewed by virtually anybody with a computer, regardless of their operating system. There are PDF reading software packages available for Windows, Apple, Linux and about any other operating system you can think of. This is why PDF is the most widely used format for an e-book, so that virtually anybody with any computer can read the document with little or no trouble.

With my Open Office Writer application that I use in creating eBooks, I can simply export the document in PDF format and I am done. Your application may be different, but you should be able to find some way of saving your document as PDF. My recommendation would be to completely finish the document – all text, images and formatting of the document in your word processing program first, before exporting as a PDF file. This way, once you do the export, everything should be done, and ready to start selling!

**Selling your eBook**

OK, the writing of the actual book is up to you. Share your expertise, no matter what the subject is. But, what about getting the dollars and cents from your book? Honestly, while many people feel scared by this part of the project, this is actually a relatively simple and straightforward process, and something that anybody can do, including you! I mean, I do it, so I am sure you can do it easily too!

There are a number of ways to accomplish this goal, and we'll look at several routes you can go. I will also let you know which way I feel is best, and why I feel it is the best too.

In order to sell an eBook, frankly, you need to be able to accept a credit card (or debit card) payment in some way. After all, your sales are going to be virtual sales, over the Internet, so there is no way to exchange the cash in a face to face setting in most cases. In my years of selling e-books, I do collect cash in exchange for a CD disc with the e-book from time to time for local buyers, but this is rare.

If you are located in the United States, or some other first world country, one of your options, particularly if you will be selling a huge volume of books, is to get a Merchant Account with your bank, which will allow you to accept credit cards online. However, in most parts of the world this is not really feasible to do, and there are other ways to accomplish the money end much easier. Also, if you are only going to be selling a few e-books each month, perhaps up to a few hundred e-books (depending on price) it is not really feasible to go with a Merchant Account, because the amount of business you will be generating is too small to mess with for most banks.

Luckily, though, for most of us, there are other online payment options. Let's look at two different ones that I use, and the pros and cons of each:

**PayPal**

Overall, for selling an e-book, I feel that PayPal

(http://www.Paypal.com) is the best solution. PayPal used to be a solution that was for the USA, and a few other big countries like the UK, Australia, etc., but these days, PayPal covers most of the world. For many years, I could not get a PayPal account, because I live in the Philippines, but for about 4 years or so now, PayPal has been serving the Philippines, and I have been very happy with their service.

With PayPal, you can expect to pay a fee of anywhere from 2% to 5% of your selling price to PayPal for their service. In addition to the percentage fee, PayPal will also charge you a fee of around 30 US cents for each transaction. The exact amount of the fee you pay depends on two factors:

- Where you are located in the world – the USA pays the lowest fees, with small countries like the Philippines and other third world countries paying more.

- The amount of volume you do. The more your consistent sales are from month to month, the lower the fee you pay will be with PayPal.

Most people are happy to pay using PayPal, but there are some people who are reluctant to use the service. Why? Mainly because they are scared to use PayPal. While PayPal is the biggest company handling online transactions, that has made them a target for fraudsters as well, with some people targeting PayPal for all sorts of schemes. Really, PayPal has done an excellent job of combating this, but some people are still scared to use the service. Personally, I use PayPal exclusively in my e-book sales off of the website. If somebody contacts me and says they want to pay in a different way, though, I do offer them other options. Thankfully, though, this is not a big problem, as the number of such requests is very small.

One thing that I find very convenient in using PayPal is that I can, at any time, transfer my money to my bank account and it is available, usually within 48 to 72 hours.

## 2Checkout

Another service that I have been using for nearly a decade now is called 2Checkout (http://www.2Checkout.com). 2Checkout offers you the ability to accept a credit card payment from any major Credit Card (MasterCard, Visa, JCB, Diners Club, etc.). The cost of using 2Checkout is 5.5% of the transaction plus a 30 cent per transaction fee.

2Checkout normally pays out your earned money every Friday each week, provided you have earned enough to reach the payment threshold, which in most cases is only $10.

A big advantage for using 2Checkout, if you live outside the USA is that they offer a lot of different ways to collect your money. They will direct deposit your money into a US bank account. If your bank account is in a different country, they will wire transfer your money to your foreign bank account. Also, a very convenient service is that they have a relationship with a company called Payoneer, which will issue you a Debit Card to use anywhere in the world. You can use the Debit Card much like a Credit Card, or by withdrawing cash at an ATM machine anywhere in the world.

I like using 2Checkout and find it convenient. However, I choose to use PayPal as my primary processor for Credit Card payments because of the ability to transfer my money to my bank at any time, not having to wait for the Friday payout that 2Checkout enforces.

**Other Processors**

There are lots of other payment processors out there too, but these are two reliable ones that I have used over the years, and I recommend each of them, depending on your needs. I find it convenient to have both available, and I use both, with PayPal as my default option, but 2Checkout as a backup for clients that prefer not to use PayPal for their online payment.

If you want to try other Payment processors, just do a Google

search for "online payment processor" and I am sure you will find dozens of other options. I cannot recommend those, because I don't use them, but I feel quite confident in the two that I do recommend, because I have used each of them for years and years now.

**Doing the transaction**

OK, so you have written a book that you want to sell as an e-book, or an electronic book on the Internet. You have chosen a company to process the payments online. But, how do you actually do the mechanics of selling the book? Frankly, there are a number of ways that you can do this.

Of course, the first step you will need to take is to set up a website to sell your book. While the actual construction of the website is outside the scope of this book, for ease of setting up, and standardization, I would recommend just going with a WordPress blog (not WordPress.com where you get a free hosted blog, but rather a blog that you host yourself using WordPress software, which is free), and then adding some sales features to that.

Your next step after setting up your website is how to be able to sell something off of your site. Regardless of what Payment Processor you elect to use, most of them will offer you the ability to put "buy now" buttons on your site. For example, you log into your PayPal account and go to the Merchant Services section and there is an option to create a "Buy Now" button for your site. While this works well, the functionality is also limited. For example, if somebody buys your e-book and pays for it, there is no way to really set up the ability for them to download the book, and you are stuck e-mailing the book to them at some later time when you are at your computer. While this will certainly work, the problem is that most people want the book "instantly" after making the payment. There are ways to do this, which we will discuss shortly.

So, no matter which Payment Processor you use, you can set up the "Buy Now" buttons very easily and add them to your site. However, if you want the ability to offer "instant download" of the book after purchase, you will need to add some other service in conjunction with PayPal or your processor of choice.

## E-Junkie

While the name is not very attractive to me, I use a company called e-Junkie to handle the sale, and they also take care of making the book instantly downloadable for the buyer. E-Junkie offers makes it easy to sell your e-book online, and takes care of customer service issues, downloads, interfacing with PayPal and other providers and just generally makes selling e-books a no brainer! I highly recommend e-Junkie for your e-book selling.

In addition to making your product instantly downloadable, eJunkie can offer you other options too. Let's have a look at some of what they can do for you:

1. Affiliate Program: e-Junkie can help you set up an affiliate program. What is an affiliate program? It lets you pay others to promote your book! So, others can put banner ads on their websites, and you pay them for books that they sell for you! You get to decide how much to pay, and any terms and conditions, but this can be set up very easily with your e-Junkie account.

2. Discount coupons and promotions: One thing I like to do from time to time is offer a special discount to my regular website readers. So, about once per month or so, I will offer a special on my websites,

and give a coupon code for my readers to enter for their book purchases. This way, my regular readers can get a special discount. I set the price of the offer, or a percentage off, right in my e-Junkie account, I can even set the dates that the coupon code is valid, and when it expires. This is very convenient, and a great way to pick up extra sales!

3. Buy Now buttons: When you use e-Junkie you don't need to worry about things like Buy Now buttons from PayPal or your other Payment Provider! That's right, e-Junkie offers their own buttons for your website. In fact, e-Junkie's buttons are much more sophisticated, and when you use them you actually get a full-fledged shopping cart system right on your website! You don't have to go to the trouble of installing shopping cart software, configuration and such, eJunkie takes care of that for you. All you have to do is put a small piece of code on your site, and you are up and running!

There are other companies offering similar services to what eJunkie is offering, but I started using e-Junkie about a year ago, and I have had nothing but praise for the service that they are offering me!

Now, remember, though, e-Junkie is not free, you will have to pay to use their service! But, it's cheap! Just sell a single e-book and in most cases you have already paid off e-Junkie's monthly charge and made some money for yourself too. E-Junkie offers a number of different levels of service, and a lot depends on how many different products you are selling, but their charge ranges starting from just $5 and can go to any amount higher than that. For me, I am selling about 20 different products, and all are downloadable direct from eJunkie's server, and I am paying $10 per month to e-Junkie for providing the service. As I said, I have had no complaints, and frankly, a lot of praise to e-Junkie for their service. Highly recommended.

**Wrapping it all up**

OK, so let's wrap it all up with a bit of a recap.

How do you sell an e-book product?

1. Write a book, based on your area of expertise.

2. Set up a website where you can sell your book, or books after you have established yourself and are offering multiple products.

3. Check out the payment processors who can assist you in taking online payments from people who are eager to buy your book.

4. Use a service like e-Junkie who will take care of all of the Administration of handling the shopping cart part of the transaction. They are cheap, easy to use, and a very valuable service.

Do these things, and you can be selling your book in minutes! Your most important job comes before you write the book. Make yourself known on the Internet for the niche area that you have expertise in. Write articles on the topic on your website. Garner a following. Create a community online of people who know you as an expert in your field, and are willing and hungry to purchase more information from you. If you do these simple things, honestly, you have the potential to sell a lot of e-books, and make some nice money over the Internet. I have done it myself, so I know it can be done.

Good luck!

# 48 – PAPERBACK BOOKS

I first started writing electronic books about 15 years ago. At that time I wrote a single book, and I didn't do any other books for probably another 7 or 8 years after that. That book that I wrote so many years ago did OK, but nothing spectacular. But, when I got back into doing eBooks, my second book was a smash hit. The first book made me, at best, $100 per month or so, and usually less than that. The second book that I did earned me more like $1,000 per month on the bad months and sometimes as much as $4-$5,000 per month. I consider that to be quite a success, especially since the book kept earning over many years. It is hard to beat that as a self-publisher and self-seller, selling your book simply through your own website.

Since coming out with that book, I have tried to continue with my success by coming out with at least one new book every year. Some years I have even come out with more than a dozen or two new eBooks, albeit usually smaller books. I find that whenever I come out with a new eBook my book earnings spike. Not only the new book, but there is usually regenerated interest in my older books as well, and the sales of all books spikes. That is why I try to come out with new books at least once every year. What I have found is that when I come out with a new book and sales are good, the sales will slowly taper off. After about a year the new book has tapered off to a consistent, but lower level of sales. So, that is why I try to time it so that I have a new book (or series of books) each year. It keeps my sales steady, regenerates interest in my older catalog, and keeps people interested.

I was an author back in the early 90s as well, but all of my books were paper books. eBooks certainly were not much of a rage at that time, I don't even recall if electronic books existed back then. In the very early 21st Century when I decided to get back into book writing, I went straight to electronic books, because that was the "in thing" to do, and also because it was very easy to produce an eBook. Profits were good, and generally it was just the way to go.

When I started coming out with electronic books, though, I would get requests from some customers for paper books. I would oblige the people by simply printing the book on my laser printer, and binding it. It was a nice print job, but certainly not of the quality of a good paperback or hard cover book. My customers understood, though, that I was just providing this service as a favor to them, so it was not going to be the highest quality book that they had ever purchased.

A few years into doing this "book printing" on my own, I finally decided that it was just too much trouble to do, and I stopped doing it. When I got requests for paper books, I just told the customer that I did not have print books available, but if they wanted to buy the eBook they were free to print it on their own printer, otherwise I was just sorry that I could not oblige them. I did this for quite a few years, and it got down to the point where I got few such requests, so I figured that everything was fine.

A while back, I looked into doing print books again. I found that there are now a lot of POD publishers. POD is Print On Demand. An example is CreateSpace, which is the company that did the printing and binding for this book. CreateSpace is owned by Amazon. I was a bit intrigued and wanted to give it a try. One of the reasons is that my online niche is comprised about 90% of older, retired people. Most people in that age group prefer a printed book that they can hold in their hands over a file that they can read on their Kindle or PC.

I sent a note to a friend who is also a writer. This friend publishes his books in both paper and electronic format. I asked him how he did with paper. This friend writes in a niche where mostly younger people read his books, so I expected that eBook sales would far exceed paperback sales. Boy, was I shocked at what he told me. When my friend replied to me he told me that he generally sells around 5 paper books for every eBook that he sells. I had read online that generally you will sell about 4 paper books for every eBook. This pretty much shocked me, and the numbers were very close to what my friend had told me.

Given the age of my average customer, I knew that I was missing the boat. It was time to take my best e-Titles and port them over to paper as well. So, I have started along this path and so far it has been very successful. From now on, whenever I release a new eBook there will be a paper version available as well.

Do you know how POD publishing works?

It is really a great process. Did you realize that you can publish a paperback book absolutely free? It's true, it will cost you nothing.

If you have already written the book for publication as an eBook you can just do a little reformatting and then go to CreateSpace or another POD publisher, upload the properly formatted file, cover art and such, and within just a couple of days your book is available in paperback too. No books are printed, so there is no cost to you. Whenever Amazon gets a sale on your paperback book, they tell the folks at CreatSpace. CreateSpace then prints the book, binds it, etc. and it is shipped out to the customer who bought the book! You never have to pay anything, and within a few days your percentage of the sale is deposited into your bank account. It is so simple, and so far I am seeing that the sales are great! I have not been doing it long enough to be able to know how it will stack up against my eBook sales, but it is looking like I will end up selling at least 3 paperbacks for every electronic book that I sell. How could I go wrong.

So, look at this carefully. I think it is a move that you should make too. There is really nothing to lose, so give it a try!

# 49 – BE A PUBLISHER

As I said in an earlier idea, you can self-publish books! You know what? If you can self-publish a book there is no reason why you can't just start a small publishing business yourself!

When other people see that you are writing and publishing books, they will be curious about that, and they will ask questions. Offer to publish a book for them, and set your price at 50% of the profit. The average that a writer would get from a big publisher is around 10%, so what you are offering is very generous if you only want 50%.

I do this, and it is very successful for me. The way that I handle it is that I charge a flat fee for my editing, formatting and publishing the work. Most of what I do with these tasks is setting up Kindle books for people. I am very well versed on how to format and publish Kindle books, but many people have a hard time doing it. Also, my son is a Photoshop expert, so he will design covers for Kindle books (or other books). So, for example, if somebody has a manuscript that they wish to sell on Kindle, they will pay my son $50 or so for the cover design. Next, I will read the book, fix errors, suggest changes, format the book properly and then set it all up on Kindle for the client. Once I have done these things, my part of the work is done, and the book author will then deal directly with Amazon.

I also offer a service where I will sell their books on my Bookstore website. If I sell the books, I get 50% of the selling price. So many people like to write, but they have no idea how to sell, or even how to prepare their work for publication. It is not hard to find these clients, in fact there are so many people in this category that if you market this service effectively you will have a lot of clients!

There are different ways to format books for Kindle, you can do a Google search and find plenty of tutorials on that on the web. In short, you can put the manuscript into Microsoft Word, and when everything is ready, just use Word to save the file as a "Web Page, Filtered" and that format is acceptable by Amazon for the Kindle Platform.

If you are preparing a book manuscript for publication on the web, that would mostly be done by saving the manuscript as a PDF file, which can also be done with Word.

It is very easy work, and also lots of demand for this kind of service. Give it a try!

# SECTION 8 - BONUS IDEA

I'm throwing in an extra way to make money!

# 50 – BONUS IDEA! SELL THIS BOOK

That's right, I told you I'd give you 49 ideas on how to earn a living without a job, but I'm going to throw in an extra one for you, and this one will benefit you and me!

**Sell this book!**

That's right, go to my website and sign up for my Affiliate Program. Then, advertise my book on your site and I will give you 25% for every book that is sold to a person who clicks through your site and buys the book within 30 days!

I told you about Affiliate Marketing earlier in the book, well, this idea is putting Affiliate Marketing to work!

So, as I said, every visitor that you send to my site to buy the book, when they purchase the book, I'm going to give you 25% of it! That's right, I did all the work of writing it, and I'm going to give you one fourth! So, go sign up today, put up a banner on your site, write a review of this book, mention it in your blog post, whatever, and include your affiliate link so that I can give you 25% for every book that you sell for me! It's that easy.

Plus, on top of that, I have dozens of other books as well, and you get 25% on any of them.

I also sell language courses to learn Tagalog or Bisaya, and you get 25% when you sell those!

Get started today! Go sign up now, and start making money!

You can get full details on my Affiliate Program here:

http://expatisland.com/affiliate-program/

# APPENDIX A – HOW DID BOB DO IT?

At the time of my writing, I have lived in the Philippines for more than 15 years. As I explained at the beginning of this book, when I came here I had what I thought was plenty of money to get my life here on track, and earn a nice living. I was wrong, though, I quickly went through that money by living in stupid ways (living like I was rich, which I am not). I came to the point that I either had to leave the country, send my wife abroad to work or figure out how to earn money here. I decided to figure out how to earn money here in the Philippines – the other two options were not even considered.

One of the reasons why I am writing this book is because I don't want you to follow my stupid footsteps. The problem is that most people that I see, expats who move to the Philippines, act even more stupidly than I did when I moved here. I don't want you to do that. The fact is, that most people do live stupidly, they run through their money way more quickly than they thought they would, and few can ever figure out how to make a living here in the Philippines. So, what happens most of the time is that these people end up having to leave the country in order to survive. That is sad, but I can assure you that it is true.

Let me take a look at each of the 49 Business ideas that I have given in the book, and I'll tell you my experience with the idea.

## 1.  Selling on eBay

Yes, I did personally do this for several years, and I made a lot of money selling on eBay. If I had not been pushed into eBay by my wife, I do not think that I would be living in the Philippines today, I may not even be self-employed any longer, and would be forced to "have a job".

## 2.  An eBay Selling Service

I have done this to some extent. While I have never formally set up a storefront for such services, I have sold items on eBay for friends and family in the past. There is demand for this service!

## 3.  Amazon FBA

FBA is a fairly new program, but I am very excited about it. While I don't have too much experience with FBA yet, I have a lot of experience selling on Amazon through other routes. I already have an FBA account, and am just at the early stages of getting my products up on Amazon. By the time this book is available to the public, my FBA selling business will be active and I believe it will be quite successful! In the next edition of this book, I hope to be able to tell you more!

## 4. Start an Amazon FBA Support Business

This is not something I have done, nor do I intend to do it. The reason? Because I am not located in the USA where I would need to be to have the best access to Amazon's warehouses so that I could adequately support FBA businesses. As an expat living abroad, I am in a position where if somebody else had such a support business I would be a customer of that business! A few such businesses do actually exist already, but the ones I have seen are mostly in Europe, and I would need something nearer to the USA Amazon system.

## 5. DS Domination

While I am not part of DS Domination, I have at least a dozen close friends who are deeply involved with DS Domination, and are all quite successful. From what I can see, if you put in the time and work necessary, there is no reason why you cannot succeed.

## 6. DVD/CD Creation

I had a number of online courses, and I had one in particular that I knew could have a wide audience, but I just had to figure out how to reach that audience. For this particular course, Amazon had nothing like it in their wide selection, so I figured that if I could get it listed on Amazon, I would have a winner, with no competition. I contemplated for about 2 years on how to get the course listed on Amazon. When I finally discovered the DVD/CD creation process at Kunaki, I knew that I had a winner. And, indeed, it has turned out to be a winner for me. I now have a number of DVD based products on Amazon, and they are good sellers for me.

## 7. Blogging

Blogging is something that I have done for many years now, and I am still doing it. I find that in addition to making money from my blogs and also because of my blogs, I also use my blogs to raise my profile, become more well known, and use that to make money in other business ventures. I expect that I will actively blog for the rest of my life.

## 8. Blog for money with sponsored posts

I personally have not blogged in a "pay per post" fashion, but I know a number of people who have been doing this. For those who are unable to make money in other ways, I believe that this method is a failsafe way to be able to earn enough to survive on wherever you live in the world.

## 9. Blog Support Business

have offered many different "blog support" type services over the years. In early 2015, though, I formalized it by starting a service called "CurvePress" that is a "Suite of WordPress Services". So far, CurvePress has been very good to me, and I believe that it will continue to offer me some excellent results in the years to come.

## 10. Set up a free blogging service with ads

I have used WordPress MU extensively, so technically I have done very similar services to this. I have yet to set it up as a free blogging service, but it is something I have thought extensively about.

## 11. e-Commerce

e-Commerce has been very good to me, today it is my number one component of my income. I have learned a lot over the years through my work in e-Commerce. Not only have I learned about doing e-Commerce, but I also learned more about all types of business, and about being a businessman. The roots of my business life are in retailing. I started in retail when I was 15 years old. I found that I was a natural born retailer, and most of my other business experiences grew out of my natural retailing abilities and the things I learned when I was active in retail, and I feel that ecommerce is a natural extension of the physical retailing world.

## 12. Build Websites

I have done dozens of website building jobs over the years for various clients. I still build websites for clients today, but I limit this business only to clients who host with me through my Web Hosting service. So, in other words, I tie the two together, and thus make more money that way.

## 13. Ask the Expert

While I don't have any sites that are specifically "Ask the Expert" sites, I have sites that are similar in nature. I offer a service, and use the moniker, "The Expat Answerman" because I answer questions for other expats on how to live the expat lifestyle successfully.

## 14. Build Websites for your Products

What can I say? This is the meat and potatoes of what I do and how I make money! I use many of the strategies in this book to build up my profile and make it possible to establish my own products. But, the rubber hits the road when I build websites to actually sell my products.

## 15. Start a website about the place where you live

You should certainly do this. It helps establish you as an expert in your area, and that can bring a lot of business! I have many such websites – even about places where I don't live! A website about the place where I live is really the entire basis of my success, so I can honestly say that this is where it all started for me, and has carried me through to great success on the Internet.

## 16. Sell indigenous products

Yes, I have done this a number of times. It is not something that you will likely be able to make into a full time job, but you can make money on it.

## 17. Web Hosting

I do have a Web Hosting service today, and have for about 8 years now. It is a good business for me, because basically there is some work involved (very little) in getting things set up, and after that it kind of goes on auto-pilot and just keeps bringing in money month after month.

## 18. Buy a website that is already making money

Again, I have never done this, but I know a lot of people who have, and I have based what I wrote on their experiences. I have no doubt that this can be an excellent strategy to establish yourself online, and get your start on the web! I have bought an existing website that was not earning money, and I turned it into a money maker that generates about $2,000 per month in revenue for me. Imagine where I could be if I had started out with something that was already making money!

## 19. Building a Community on the Internet

This is a place where I have a GREAT DEAL of experience! I have actually built more than one thriving community site on the Internet, and while the actual community site may not turn out to be a money maker, it give you the opportunity to use other sites to make a great deal of money! This is a BIG winner!

## 20. Make Membership Sites

Once you have built a community, like I outlined in Chapter 18, the next logical step is to start building things like Membership sites, and they can literally rake in the money! Some people make tens of thousands of dollars per month through monthly memberships to some of their sites. I do not make that much through membership, but I make many hundreds of dollars each month with this method. Nothing wrong with that, and it keeps growing each month!

## 21. Affiliate Marketing

Yes, I have done this, although only with mixed success. There are a lot of people who are very successful at this, though, so there is no doubt that it can be done.

## 22. Graphic Design Business

While I haven't done this myself, I know others who do it successfully. My son is just getting into this business, he is 18 years old. He has a real eye and a talent for graphic design, especially using Photoshop. I intend to use him for my graphic design needs, and that will help promote him to my large online audience.

## 23. Take on Jobs from Overseas

I have done this to an extent, but have never gone all out trying to drum up business. There is business out there, and if you push to get it, you can do very well.

## 24. Offer a Course on Udemy

I started offering courses on Udemy in 2014 and early 2015. So far, it is making money, but not enough to live on. It makes money that supplements or adds to my existing income, which is still nice. However, it is important to remember that my courses on Udemy are very narrow niches at this time. Nothing that would draw a diverse audience. Serving a niche like this has benefits but also drawbacks. The benefit is that I have no competition on Udeny, so far at least. The disadvantage is that there is not a crowd who wants to take my course. That is OK, though, because it is what I expected, and the courses that I have been offering to date are designed more to give me experience and learn about how Udemy works, so that I can apply that knowledge when I go for a larger more diverse course at a later date.

## 25. Offer Courses on your own Website

This is another great advantage of Udemy, and it is something that I am taking advantage of. You see, when you offer a course on Udemy, you still retain full rights and ownership of that course, and you can then put it up on your own website as well as Udemy. Since my website has a lot of traffic from within my niche, I actually have more students on my own website than on Udemy. Another big advantage of offering the course on your own site is that you get 100% of the money, and don't have to share it with Udemy or their affiliates. I highly recommend making courses and then multitasking your courses by offering them in more than one location. It works well for me.

## 26. Create Website Templates

I can't say that I have done this for money, although I have created plenty of templates, it is usually for myself or friends. I have been on the buying end of this business many times, though. I noted in an earlier paragraph that my son was starting a graphic design business. Another aspect of his business is producing website templates and themes. Since I try to help my son as much as possible, I will be gaining a lot more experience in this particular way to make a living. I hope I have more to report in the next edition of this book!

## 27. App Development

Apps are the gold mine of this time! The Gold Rush that happened in California in 1849 is about what is going on these days for Apps. Apps for phones, tablets, even for Windows. If you know how to program for Apps, and have a creative mind, this is a great way to make money. Unfortunately, I am not a programmer, but again, this is something that my son is working on, and hoping to become proficient. A lot of things that I am not educated on in the field of tech are things that my son is learning, and I believe that in the future we will complement each other very well, and make a great team!

## 28. Multitask your products

If you only take one idea from this book and run with it, please.. take this one! I personally believe that this is the best idea that you can run with and do very well. Of course, I also believe that you need to take many of the other ideas in the book, and then apply this idea to each of them. Put everything you do to multiple tasks and use the ideas in multiple ways. This is what I do, and you can do the work one time and use it to make money in many different ways. Multitasking is the key to your ultimate success!

## 29. Buy a Franchise

As I pointed out, I have done this, but I found out that it is not a good move for a person of my personality type. If you are a person who can follow instructions, go for it! It is a proven business strategy.

## 30. Consulting

When I wrote the first edition of this book, I recommended trying consulting, but I also said that it was not something that I had done. Well, in the years since the first release of this book, I have turned consulting into one of the cornerstones of my business. I have also used things like my book writing to augment my consulting. The books give me authority that makes it where people want to hire me as a consultant, and also much of what is in the books is what people ask me about, and I already have the answers for their questions ready to go. If you can get into consulting, I highly recommend this.

## 31. Teach English

I personally do not have the patience to be a good teacher, but there are a lot of people doing this successfully here in the Philippines. There are so many Koreans coming here to learn English, that starting this business is very easy!

## 32. Write a newsletter

If you are successful at blogging or have built an audience in another way, this is a must. I send out different newsletters to different niches just about every single day. I have used it to build up a nice list of names that I can market to.

## 33. Line up mundane computer jobs

Yes, I have done this, and with terrific results! I highly recommend doing this every time you get a chance!

## 34. Balikbayan Box Service

I have not done this as a business, although there have been a number of times that I have had people send me Balikbayan Boxes with stuff that I need or want. I have surveyed up to 100 expats here, and have always been told that it is a service that they would use. If you set up this kind of business, let me know and I will sign up as your first customer!

## 35. Fill your own needs

Every time that I have gotten items shipped to me from the States, other expats say "I'd sure like to get some of that" so I have no doubt that this is a winning business idea. I have not done it for money so far, but I know it will work!

## 36. Private Investigative Service

I do this regularly, and I know that there is demand for it, because I get e-mails almost daily from people who want to scrounge up information here in the Philippines.

## 37. Sell Real Estate for a commission

My wife, Feyma, has been doing this for years now, and very successfully! This has turned into one of our largest money making initiatives. Of course, it is up and down, but when it is "up" there is a ton of money to be made.

## 38. Put your expertise to work!

I do this all the time! This is something that can apply to every idea in the book!

## 39. Translation work

Unfortunately, I only speak two languages, and one of them is a little used language. So, I have not done this myself, but I have a good friend who does this as a full time job here in the Philippines.

## 40. Tour Services

I do this all the time, although in more of a casual way, nothing formalized. I know that I could make more money doing this if I set up a formal business and advertise my services.

## 41. Turn a Hobby into a Business

This is something that I have done successfully all the way back to the 1980's. You can do it too!

## 42. Do a monthly Conference Call

I do this, but only on occasion. I know others who do this and make a ton of money doing it.

## 43. Buy Properties, fix them up, and flip

So far, I have not tried this, although I know others who have been successful with this strategy.

## 44. Build an Apartment Complex

This is something that I have been researching heavily lately, and it is something that I intend to do in the not-so-distant future. There is a bundle to be made with this business.

## 45. Do what you are passionate about

While this is not a specific idea, I believe that this is one the most premium pieces of advice in this book. This is the first advice that I give to every person who asks me how to make money. In this book, this will be one of the last ideas that I give, because the final ideas tend to make the most impact when you are reading a book. When you do what you are passionate about, the money will always find you!

## 46. Think outside the box

Thinking outside the box is the key to success in any field, in my opinion. If you combine this idea with any other idea in this book, in my opinion, you cannot fail.

## 47. Write eBooks

I'm doing this right now, and have been doing for many years now! I have more than 100 books in the past 25 years. So, with my experience I know that you can succeed here. In the 90s I wrote books which were paper based. Over the past 10 years or so, I have been writing eBooks. I am in the process of changing that, though, which you will see in idea #48.

## 48. Make your books into paperbacks

As I said earlier, I have been writing eBooks exclusively in the 2000s. In 2015, after doing some research and seeing that there is still great potential in paper based books, I decided that I will bring my most popular titles to Paperback as well as electronic. I see no reason why this will not be a big success.

## 49. Be a publisher

During the past 10 years or so I have gotten inquiries from a lot of people who want to write books. Because of the inquires, I started publishing those books for others, and I take a commission from each book that I publish. If I sell the book for the author as well, I get another commission. It works for me, and no reason why it can't work for you too!

So, now you have some solid concrete ideas on exactly what I have done to succeed in the Philippines. I hope that these help you find your own success!

*Good luck in your quest!*

# APPENDIX B – RESOURCES

Listed below are resources that I have mentioned in the book, and how to get them.

Websites

eBay: This is a premier online auction marketplace. You can find it at: http://www.ebay.com

Problogger: Website operated by Darren Rouse with plenty of suggestions of how to earn money online (particularly through blogging). http://www.ProBlogger.net

Google AdSense: A service that will place advertising on your blog or website. http://www.google.com/adsense

Chitika: A service that will place advertising on your blog or website. http://www.chitika.com

Text Link Ads: A service that will place text advertising on your blog or website. http://matomyseo.com

OSCommerce: Shopping cart software for use in an online store or e-commerce site. I highly recommend this shopping cart software. http://www.oscommerce.com

PayPal: A service that can be used to send money online. In addition, PayPal can be integrated with your online shopping cart as a payment solution, allowing your customers to pay with their credit cards, or their PayPal account. I recommend this as your primary payment solution, and a way to get money from your customers overseas for any reason at all. http://www.paypal.com

2Checkout: Another Payment Processor that I use extensively and recommend highly. I have been using 2Checkout for about 6 or 7 years now, and they have always been fair to me and my customers. http://www.2checkout.com

ServInt: A premium webhosting company. I have used ServInt for years and their service is great. http://www.servint.net

Solostream: A great service that makes Website templates (particularly WordPress). http://www.solostream.com

Linkshare: An affiliate marketing service where you can sign up for many affiliate programs to use on your website. http://http://marketing.rakuten.com/

Commission Junction: An affiliate marketing service similar to Linkshare. http://www.commissionjunction.com

RK Franchise: My friend's company that offers franchise services in the Philippines. The owner is my friend, Rudolf Kotik, and I recommend him highly. http://www.rkfranchise.com

John T. Reed: An expert in the area of Self-Publishing. I recommend his work highly, and particularly his book on the subject of self-publishing. http://www.johntreed.com

Additional Resources

# Bob's Websites

## Philippine Related Sites:

Live in the Philippines

http://LiveInThePhilippines.com

Live in the Philippines Real Estate

http://LiveInThePhilippines.net

Live in the Philippines Services Directory

http://LiveInThePhilippines.org

Live in the Philippines Consulting

http://LiveInThePhilippines.asia

How to Move to the Philippines

http://HowToMoveToThePhilippines.com/

Your Philippine Visa

http://YourPhilippineVisa.com

Get Philippine Citizenship

http://GetPhilippineCitizenship.com

Learn a Philippine Language

http://LearnAPhilippineLanguage.com

Mindanao Magazine

http://Mindanao.com

Philippine Dual Citizenship

http://PhilippineDualCitizenship.com

Pointman PI – Philippine Investigations

http://PointmanPI.com

Ride the Jeepney

http://RideTheJeepney.com

**Other Sites:**

MindanaoBob (Personal Site)

http://MindanaoBob.com

Ways to Make a Living

http://WaysToMakeALiving.com

CurvePress - Suite of WordPress Services

http://CurvePress.com

**Commerce Sites:**

Bob's Bookstore

http://ExpatIsland.com

WowPhilippines

http://WowPhilippines.com

Load Me Now

http://loadmenow.com

# ABOUT THE AUTHOR

Bob Martin is an American, but has been living in the Philippines since 2000. Bob is a Serial Entrepreneur. He starts new kinds of businesses on an ongoing basis. Bob is a big believer in what he calls "Streams of Income". Instead of having a single job or business to earn money, Bob believes that it is much wiser to have many small streams of income. By doing that, if one stream dries up, it has little effect on the overall river of income that is created by the streams, because there are still many small streams feeding the river. That one stream of income that dried up is only a small part of the overall picture, so the river will still supply your needs. Bob has written many books, mostly on the topics of Amateur Radio, Living the Expat Life, and Business topics.

Printed in Great Britain
by Amazon